Fitness Testing 101

Fitness Testing 101

A Guide for Personal Trainers and Coaches.

Patrick S. Hagerman, Ed.D.

iUniversity Press

San Jose New York Lincoln Shanghai

Fitness Testing 101
A Guide for Personal Trainers and Coaches.
All Rights Reserved © 2001 by Patrick S. Hagerman

iUniversity Press
an imprint of iUniverse.com, Inc.

For information address:
iUniverse.com, Inc.
5220 S 16th, Ste. 200
Lincoln, NE 68512
www.iuniverse.com

ISBN: 0-595-16806-X

Printed in the United States of America

Contents

List of Illustrations

List of Tables

Preface

In the past, fitness testing was reserved for researchers in a laboratory setting. Today personal trainers and athletic coaches also use fitness testing with their clients and athletes. People that hire personal trainers are usually interested in seeing specific results and have specific goals. Athletes have performance goals that must be met and improved upon each season. The best way to determine progress toward these goals is to perform fitness testing to establish a baseline reference point; and again later in the program to measure progress or change.

The tests included in this text were chosen because they did not require expensive and specialized equipment, were easy to administer, and most have some type of norms to compare against. Therefore, you do not need to have a degree in exercise physiology, have taken classes in laboratory techniques, or have a lot of special tools to administer these tests.

Fitness testing is not only used for measuring progress. If used as part of an initial consultation and pre-exercise screening, testing can help you to determine in what areas a person needs to concentrate their training. This information can assist you in better preparing a comprehensive workout program that meets the specific needs of each client or athlete.

Performing fitness testing requires more than just a battery of tests and measures. Examinees must be carefully screened before administering a test to reduce any possible complications during the test. The administration of the test requires precise set-up, process and measurement to ensure accurate results. Finally, the interpretation of the results must be done in the context of each specific examinee to provide them with relevant information.

The skills needed to perform pre-test screenings, test selection and administration, and interpretation of the results are usually taught in college classes or found in various textbooks. This manual was designed and written for those of us working in the physical education, coaching and personal training fields, and will take you step by step through the process.

The first chapter describes the entire process of fitness testing; including pre-test screening methods and tools, how to select an appropriate test depending on the results of the pre-test screening and the examinee's goals, where and when testing should take place within an exercise program, and finally how to administer fitness tests so that you get useable data.

The remainder of the book is a collection of fitness tests, categorized into chapters on cardiovascular endurance, muscular strength and endurance, power, speed, flexibility, agility, kinesthesis, balance, reaction, and body composition. Each chapter provides detailed descriptions of each test, photos and illustrations of the testing procedure, and tables of data to help you classify the fitness level of your examinee.

This book was written for the following audiences:
- Personal Trainers working with general population clients
- Personal Trainers working with high-school, collegiate, or professional athletes
- High school, collegiate, or professional Strength and Conditioning coaches
- Laboratory manual for collegiate Exercise Physiology courses

Acknowledgements

I would especially like to thank my beautiful wife Becki for her support and contributions to this project, and putting up with my late nights and weekend work. Also, the help of Dr. Frank Kulling and Dr. Tom Altena in finding, editing, and providing feedback on the various tests and data. Thanks also to those who served as models for the photos, and were patient until I got just the right shot

Chapter 1:

The Who, What, Where, When and How of Fitness Testing

The ultimate goal of any client or athlete is to improve their fitness or sport performance. The only true way of understanding whether a training program is having the desired effect is to measure the changes that take place over the course of the training program. Testing your clients and athletes will give you feedback that you can use to make modifications to the training program so that goals are met.

WHO:

Fitness testing can be performed on almost any client or athlete provided careful screening has been done. The most obvious contraindication to performing any type of fitness test is pain experienced during the movements required of the test. If your client or athlete indicates that a specific movement or position causes them pain, do not perform any tests that include that movement or position. For instance, if a client normally has knee pain after running for any length of time, testing them for speed or running endurance would not be suggested.

A pre-test health screening should always be performed because some contraindications may not be as apparent as pain. The screening can consist of a comprehensive physical exam performed by a physician, or a health history questionnaire, or both. A screening questionnaire should cover any possible problems or contraindications to exercise. The following questions should be included in any screening questionnaire, but may not include all the information you need to ask depending on your facility's requirements and policies:

1. Has your doctor ever said you have heart trouble or any cardiovascular problems?

2. Do you frequently suffer from pains in your chest, or have chest pain during physical activity?

3. Have you ever suffered a heart attack?

4. Have you ever suffered a stroke?

5. Do you ever experience an irregular or racing heart during exercise or while at rest?

6. Do you often feel faint or have spells of dizziness?

7. Has a doctor ever said that your blood pressure is too high (systolic >140, diastolic >90)?

8. Do you often have difficulty breathing?

9. Do you have asthma?

10. Has a doctor ever told you that you have a bone or joint problem such as arthritis that has been aggravated by exercise, or might be aggravated with exercise?

11. Are you a male over 45 years of age, or a woman over 55 years of age, and not accustomed to vigorous exercise?

12. Are you diabetic?

13. Are you pregnant?

14. Do you smoke?

15. Has a doctor ever told you that you have high cholesterol (>240 mg/dl)?

16. Does anyone in your immediate family have a history of coronary or other atherosclerotic disease prior to age 55?

17. Are you taking any medications for a blood pressure or heart condition?

18. Is there a good physical reason not mentioned here that would prevent you from following an activity program even if you wanted to?

A positive answer to any of these questions is grounds for referring the client or athlete to a medical professional for further evaluation prior to fitness testing. If you have any doubts about the answers provided in the questionnaire, seek the advice of the client or athlete's personal physician. Obtaining medical clearance before performing fitness testing on anyone that is questionable is the only safe and responsible course of action. Once medical clearance is granted, it is also advisable to provide the physician with a description of the fitness tests that you plan to administer, and seek any input or recommendations that the physician feels is warranted.

If there are no positive answers to any of the screening questions, and there is no physical pain or other apparent reason why fitness testing cannot be performed, or if you have medical clearance, then the next step is to decide what tests to perform.

WHAT:

Deciding which tests to perform, following acceptable pre-test screening, involves knowing the client's specific goals, or the athlete's performance needs. Personal trainers need to first find out what the client feels are his or her weaknesses, and compare these to the client's goals. If the client feels that upper body strength is an area they need to work, then testing upper body strength would be indicated. Coaches should determine what aspects of fitness are most important for the athlete's sport, and test these. For instance, a football lineman would benefit from testing for power, but not so much from cardiovascular endurance.

Another approach is to determine a battery of tests for each client or athlete that will provide an overall picture of fitness. Regardless of the client's predetermined goals, or the athlete's sport-specific needs, testing all areas of fitness can provide important information to the trainer or coach. Finding areas of weakness that can be integrated into a training program will undoubtedly produce an overall better fitness level for the client or athlete. Performing fitness testing can help to introduce the importance of a well-rounded training program to a person that is set on training only a specific fitness component. As an example, the client that spends two minutes stretching at the end of an hour workout would be well served to understand how their flexibility was rated compared to their strength. This might help them to try and incorporate more flexibility training into their program. Likewise, the marathon runner that tests poorly on muscular strength may be inclined to add more strength training into their routine.

Once you have decided which areas to test, you have to decide which of the available tests to use. Within each chapter are at least two different methods of testing a specific component of fitness. Coaches should determine which of the tests most closely mimics the athlete's sport. There may be several movements within a sport performance that can be tested independently. For instance, a football lineman can be tested for speed, agility, and power specific to that sport position. A personal trainer should choose the test that best fits the needs and abilities of the client. A person that is interested in training for marathons, would be best served by a fitness test that includes walking or running because a cycle or step test for cardiovascular endurance would not utilize the specific muscle patterns that they are training. In some cases, you may use all the different tests in a section so that you can get a better picture of where there may be strengths or weaknesses. Sometimes, performing several similar tests can help the client or athlete improve through repetition.

Overall, determining which fitness tests to use is a matter of understanding the benefits and restrictions of each test, and how each one can figure into the training program you have in mind. Once you have decided on a test, you must prepare a place to administer it properly.

WHERE:

The first consideration in choosing a location to administer a fitness test is the safety of the client or athlete. Before you conduct any test, the location or facility must meet minimum safety requirements in case of an accident. Fitness testing is not without its downsides. There is always the risk of injury, a cardiovascular or cerebrovascular accident, or death. Even with careful screening, accidents do happen. How prepared you are to handle them is the first thing that must be considered before conducting any tests.

The location should include access to a phone for dialing the emergency medical system, a first aid kit for minor cuts and scrapes, and ice packs to help reduce swelling. It is also a good idea to have another person present to assist you in case of an accident. While these precautions are probably not necessary in the case of all the tests included in this text, it is prudent to be cautious and err on the conservative side.

After the safety consideration is taken care of, the proper location for each test must be found. The tests that involve fitness equipment will probably take place in a health club or weight room. In this case, make sure that the equipment is well maintained and functioning properly, there are no obstacles nearby that may impede the client or athlete, and that bystanders are kept at a distance. For best results, the temperature and humidity of the room should be as comfortable as possible and similar to the conditions that the person normally trains in.

Outdoor tests are best performed on a track that is well maintained. If a track is not available, a marked street that doesn't experience much traffic would be acceptable. Again, obstacles should be removed, and bystanders kept at a distance. Outdoor testing should also be performed in a comfortable temperature and humidity. You may have to schedule testing for morning or evening times during summer months to protect against any heat injuries; and during the middle of the day during winter months to protect against cold injuries.

WHEN:

The timing of tests often determines how well a person performs each test. Administer tests at the same time of day that the person usually trains. Scheduling tests early in the morning for a person that usually trains in the afternoon or evening may result in lower test scores. If only one fitness test is going to be used, schedule the testing day 2-3 days after their last workout to allow for complete recovery. The best-case scenario for administering a battery of tests would allow for the testing of a different fitness component on sequential days. If this is not possible, the sequence of tests should follow a pattern that allows for complete recovery of all the energy systems between each test. Begin with the tests that do not involve much energy followed by those tests that use successively more energy and require longer recovery times. If you will be administering a test from each of the sections of this text, a logical sequence would be: body composition, flexibility, balance, kinesthesis, reaction, agility, power, muscular strength and endurance, speed, and cardiovascular.

One of the most important benefits of fitness testing is the ability to reproduce the test later to measure the changes that have taken place with a training program. It is important to recreate the testing environment exactly as it was at the time of the original baseline test; including the time of day, and for women, during the same period in the menstruation cycle.

HOW:

The actual administration of a fitness test is probably the most difficult part. Obtaining results that accurately reflect the abilities of the client or athlete requires strict adherence to the procedures for each test. Before you administer any test, read through the instructions to make sure you have the equipment and facilities to provide the proper testing setup. Organize the testing area and walk through each of the steps yourself, and then with the client or athlete to make sure that there are no questions about what is expected. Often, letting a client or athlete move through the testing procedure as sort of a trial run will reduce errors and produce a better score.

There may be times when you will have to prematurely end the test. If there is any equipment malfunction during the test, stop and make necessary repairs before re-starting the test. If the client becomes uneasy, lightheaded or experiences any pain during the test, stop immediately and follow proper first-aid procedures. If mistakes are made during the test that jeopardize the score, stop and evaluate whether to re-start or reschedule for another day.

If each of these steps is followed in order, and all procedures are correctly administered, you will have test scores that can be used to help you organize a training program that best fits each client or athlete, and gives you data that allows comparison of test-retest results to measure the program's success.

Chapter 2:

Cardiovascular / Aerobic Endurance Tests

Quite possibly the most important aspect of overall health and fitness is a person's cardiovascular conditioning. Having a high level of cardiovascular endurance enables a person to complete a wide range of activities at a high intensity level. In order to administer these tests and explain them thoroughly to your clients and athletes, it is important to understand what cardiovascular endurance is, and what can affect it.

Cardiovascular endurance refers to both the ability of the heart to pump blood, and the system of arteries, blood vessels, and veins to move blood through the body at a given level of exercise. How much blood the heart can move is called cardiac output, and is the product of heart rate and stroke volume. A person's maximal heart rate is the fastest rate that the heart can possibly beat under strenuous conditions. The only way to determine true maximal heart rate is by subjecting the examinee to a maximal stress test. Since this is a very taxing way to find maximal heart rate, an estimated maximal heart rate is more commonly used in fitness testing. Calculate estimated maximal heart rate by subtracting an examinee's age from 220. Remember that this is only an estimate. Some people will not be able to reach this heart rate, while others may be able to exceed it.

The second factor in cardiac output is stroke volume; which is the amount of blood the heart pumps out with each beat. Unfortunately, stroke volume can only be measured with sophisticated laboratory equipment. As cardiovascular endurance increases, stroke volume typically increases as well. When this occurs, resting heart rate will decrease. A person with a high level of cardiovascular fitness will have a low resting heart rate and a high resting stroke volume. The result is that the heart does not have to work as hard, or beat as many times, to move the required amount of blood.

The fitness tests included in this text use the term "estimated VO2 max" as the measure of cardiovascular endurance. VO2 Max is the greatest amount of oxygen that a person can take in and use under the most strenuous conditions. VO2 Max is expressed in units of "ml/kg/min" or milliliters of oxygen per kilogram of body weight per minute. This is actually how much oxygen the body is using each minute for each kilogram of body weight.

Testing cardiovascular endurance, and determining VO2 Max, is often done after a person has experienced some sort of cardiac event, such as a heart attack. These types of tests are usually maximal treadmill tests, overseen by a physician, and performed to determine future risk of additional cardiac problems. Maximal tests require that the person exercise to complete volitional fatigue in an attempt to make the heart work as hard as it possibly can. Having a client or athlete to perform this type of test is generally not recommended unless a physician is present.

The tests described here are sub-maximal tests. They only require the examinee to reach between 65 and 85 percent of their maximal heart rate. Most healthy people can exercise at this level, even if only for a short time. From the data that is collected, an estimate of their maximal VO2 level can be calculated. It is important to remember that the VO2 level achieved on one test may not be equal to the VO2 level achieved on a different test. The type of test used often has a lot to do with how well an examinee performs. Often the best estimates of VO2 max come from performing several tests and averaging the results.

There are three different types of tests described in this chapter: stationary cycling tests, run/walk tests, and step tests. Which test you use will depend on your evaluation of the examinee, their goals, and your determination of which test is most appropriate for them. As with all fitness testing, the test you use should be the one that most closely fits the goals of the examinee. For example, if the examinee is training for a 10K run, choosing a step test would not be the most appropriate. You should choose from the tests which most closely mimic the 10K run; which would be the 12 minute run/walk test and the 1.5 mile run test.

Choosing a cardiovascular endurance test will also depend on the abilities of the examinee. If they aren't able to run, a stationary cycle or step test would be more appropriate. If he/she is not accustomed to performing on a step, the stationary cycle may be more appropriate. You may also choose to have the examinee perform more than one cardiovascular endurance test. This is a good way of determining individual strengths on different exercises.

The results from each of these tests, except for the Harvard Step Test, will be compared to Table 2.2; which defines standard fitness levels depending on VO2 Max, age and gender. You will notice that men typically have higher VO2 Max levels for each age group. Men typically have a greater amount of lean body tissue and muscle mass than women; which results in a greater use of oxygen at any given level of exercise. VO2 Max levels also decline as you get older. This is a result of both decreasing muscle mass, and reduced ability to circulate blood because of a decreased maximal heart rate.

You will be able to make appropriate exercise prescriptions from the results of your cardiovascular endurance testing. For those examinees that score in the Low, Fair, or Average categories, cardiovascular conditioning should be a priority. For those that score Good or Excellent, you may wish to either have them train the cardiovascular system in different ways, or concentrate on other areas of their fitness program.

ASTRAND-RHYMING CYCLE TEST

For additional information see references 4, 8, 9, 17, 20

Equipment: Stationary or Recumbent cycle, Metronome or RPM readout on cycle, Stopwatch, Stethoscope, Body weight scale

Objective: To determine estimated VO2 max.

Procedure:

Adjusting the seat of the cycle: Adjust the seat height (or distance if using a recumbent) by having the examinee place the heel of their dominant foot on the pedal when the leg is fully extended and in its lowest (or farthest) position. If done correctly, when they place the ball of their foot on the pedal in this same position, there should be a slight bend in the leg at the knee. This is the correct seat height and foot placement for using a stationary or recumbent cycle. See Figures 2.1 and 2.2.

Pedaling Speed: If the cycle has a revolutions-per-minute (RPM) readout, have the examinee pedal at 50 RPM. If using a metronome, set it at 100 beats per minute, and instruct the examinee to pedal at the pace of one down-stroke for each beat.

Workload: A single workload will be used for the entire test. The workload should be set as follows:

Unconditioned or Untrained:	Women: 50–75 Watts, Men: 50—100 Watts
Conditioned or Trained:	Women: 75–100 Watts, Men: 100 – 150 Watts

Figure 2.1—Stationary cycle seat positioning—LEFT: Adjust the seat so that the leg is fully extended with the heel of the dominant foot on the pedal in its lowest position. RIGHT: Place the ball of the foot on the pedal in its lowest position. The leg should now be slightly bent at the knee.

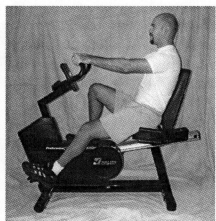

Figure 2.2—Recumbent cycle seat positioning—LEFT: Adjust the seat so that the leg is fully extended with the heel of the dominant foot on the pedal in its farthest position. RIGHT: Place the ball of the foot on the pedal in its farthest position. The leg should now be slightly bent at the knee.

Test:

1) Have the examinee warm-up by pedaling at 50 RPM for 1 minute with no workload.

2) Apply the appropriate workload and start the stopwatch. The examinee should pedal at a constant pace of 50 rpm for six minutes. Use the stopwatch to measure the minute intervals of the test.

3) Use the stethoscope to measure the examinee's heart rate during the last 20 seconds of each minute. Multiply the number of heartbeats measured during the 20-second period by 3 to obtain the heart rate per minute. Record heart rate on Datasheet #1. (If the examinee's heart rate is below 130 or above 150 beats per minute during the exercise, the workload should be increased or decreased by 25 Watts respectively).

4) At the end of the sixth minute, have the examinee continue to exercise while you compare the heart rates for the last two minutes. If they are not within five beats per minute of each other, continue the

exercise and monitor heart rate an additional minute or more until two consecutive counts are within 5 beats per minute of each other. The goal is to let the heart rate level out before ending the test.

5) At the end of the test, remove the workload and have the examinee continue pedaling for 5 minutes to cool down.

Scoring: Use Datasheet #1

1) Average the last two heart rates (those that were within 5 beats per minute of each other).

2) Compare the averaged heart rate and the final exercise workload to Table 2.3 (men) or Table 2.4 (women) to find VO2 for that workload.

3) Multiply VO2 amount by 1000.

4) Divide by the examinee's body weight in Kg (Kg = pounds / 2.2).

5) Multiply by the age correction factor using the closest age in Table 2.1.

6) Compare estimated VO2 max to Table 2.2.

Example:

A 40 year old, 154 lb. male examinee had heart rates of 145 and 147 during the last two minutes, and was exercising at a workload of 150 Watts.

1) *Average the heart rates:* 145+147 / 2 = 146 beats per minute.

2) *Compare heart rate of 146 and workload of 150W to table 2.3:* VO2 = 3.3.

3) *Multiply VO2 by 1000:* 3.3 x 1000 = 3300.

4) *Divide by weight in kg (kg = lb/2.2 = 70):* 3300/70 = 47.14

5) *Multiply by age correction factor in Table 2.1:* 47.14 x 0.83 = 39.13

6) *Compare to Table 2.2:* VO2 of 39.13 = Average

Table 2.1

Age Correction Factor for Astrand Rhyming Cycle Test
(Use closest age)

Age	Correction Factor
15	1.10
25	1.00
35	0.87
40	0.83
45	0.78
50	0.75
55	0.71
60	0.68
65	0.65

* Data from Astrand, I. (1960)

Table 2.2

Norms for Estimated Maximal Oxygen Consumption
VO2 (ml/kg/min)

Age	Low	Fair	Average	Good	Excellent
Male					
18-25	<31	31-37	38-49	50-59	>59
26-35	<28	28-36	37-45	46-54	>54
36-45	<26	26-33	34-40	41-52	>52
46-55	<23	23-30	31-38	39-46	>46
56-65	<22	22-28	29-35	36-42	>42
66+	<19	19-24	25-31	32-37	>37
Female					
18-25	<27	27-37	38-46	47-56	>56
26-35	<25	25-33	34-44	45-53	>53
36-45	<22	22-30	31-37	38-45	>45
46-55	<20	20-26	27-33	34-41	>41
56-65	<18	18-23	24-30	31-37	>37
66+	<16	16-21	22-26	27-32	>32

*Data from deVries (1986)

Table 2.3
Predicted maximal oxygen uptake (VO2 l/min) from Heart rate and Workload during Astrand-Rhyming Cycle Test for Men

Heart Rate	Workload (Watts) 50W	100W	150W	Heart Rate	Workload (Watts) 50W	100W	150W
120	2.2	3.5	4.8	142		2.5	3.5
121	2.2	3.4	4.7	143		2.5	3.4
122	2.2	3.4	4.6	144		2.5	3.4
123	2.1	3.4	4.6	145		2.4	3.4
124	2.1	3.3	4.5	146		2.4	3.3
125	2.0	3.2	4.4	147		2.4	3.3
126	2.0	3.2	4.4	148		2.4	3.2
127	2.0	3.1	4.3	149		2.3	3.2
128	2.0	3.1	4.2	150		2.3	3.2
129	1.9	3.0	4.2	151		2.3	3.1
130	1.9	3.0	4.1	152		2.3	3.1
131	1.9	2.9	4.0	153		2.2	3.0
132	1.8	2.9	4.0	154		2.2	3.0
133	1.8	2.8	3.9	155		2.2	3.0
134	1.8	2.8	3.9	156		2.2	2.9
135	1.7	2.8	3.8	157		2.1	2.9
136	1.7	2.7	3.8	158		2.1	2.9
137	1.7	2.7	3.7	159		2.1	2.8
138	1.6	2.7	3.7	160		2.1	2.8
139	1.6	2.6	3.6				
140	1.6	2.5	3.6				
141		2.6	3.5				

* Data from Astrand, I. (1960)

Table 2.4

Predicted maximal oxygen uptake VO2 (l/min) from heart rate and workload during Astrand-Rhyming Cycle Test for Women

Heart Rate	Workload (Watts)			Heart Rate	Workload (Watts)		
	50W	75W	100W		50W	75W	100W
120	2.6	3.4	4.1	142	1.7	2.3	2.8
121	2.5	3.3	4.0	143	1.7	2.2	2.7
122	2.5	3.2	3.9	144	1.7	2.2	2.7
123	2.4	3.1	3.9	145	1.6	2.2	2.7
124	2.4	3.1	3.8	146	1.6	2.2	2.6
125	2.3	3.0	3.7	147	1.6	2.1	2.6
126	2.3	3.0	3.6	148	1.6	2.1	2.6
127	2.2	2.9	3.5	149		2.1	2.6
128	2.2	2.8	3.5	150		2.0	2.5
129	2.2	2.8	3.4	151		2.0	2.5
130	2.1	2.7	3.4	152		2.0	2.5
131	2.1	2.7	3.4	153		2.0	2.4
132	2.0	2.7	3.3	154		2.0	2.4
133	2.0	2.6	3.2	155		1.9	2.4
134	2.0	2.6	3.2	156		1.9	2.3
135	2.0	2.6	3.1	157		1.9	2.3
136	1.9	2.5	3.1	158		1.8	2.3
137	1.9	2.5	3.0	159		1.8	2.2
138	1.8	2.4	3.0	160		1.8	2.2
139	1.8	2.4	2.9				
140	1.8	2.4	2.8				
141	1.8	2.3	2.8				

* Data from Astrand, I. (1960)

YMCA PHYSICAL WORKING CAPACITY TEST

For additional information see references 4, 20, 36

Equipment: Stationary or Recumbent cycle, Body weight scale, Metronome or rpm readout on cycle, Stopwatch, Stethoscope

Objective: To determine estimated VO2 max.

Procedure:

Adjusting the seat of the cycle: Adjust the seat height (or distance if using a recumbent) by having the examinee place the heel of their dominant foot on the pedal when the leg is fully extended and in its lowest (or far-thest) position. If done correctly, when they place the ball of their foot on the pedal in this same position, there should be a slight bend in the leg at the knee. This is the correct seat height and foot placement for using a sta-tionary or recumbent cycle. See Figures 2.1 and 2.2.

Pedaling Speed: If the cycle has a revolutions-per-minute (RPM) readout, have the examinee pedal at 50 RPM. If using a metronome, set it at 100 beats per minute, and instruct the examinee to pedal at the pace of one down-stroke for each beat.

Workload: The initial workload is 25 Watts. The workloads for the second, third, and fourth stages (if needed) depend on the examinee's heart rate at the end of the first stage. Table 2.5 outlines the workload progression.

Table 2.5

YMCA Physical Working Capacity Test workloads (Watts)

1st Workload = 25 Watts

	HR < 80	HR 80-89	HR 90-100	HR>100
2nd Workload	125 W ▼	100 W ▼	75 W ▼	50 W ▼
3rd Workload	150 W ▼	125 W ▼	100 W ▼	75 W ▼
4th Workload	175 W	150 W	125 W	100 W

*Modified to Watts from Golding (1989)

Test:

1) Have the examinee warm-up by pedaling at 50 rpm for 1 minute with no workload.

2) For the first stage, increase the workload to 25 Watts, and start the stopwatch.

3) Using the stethoscope, record the examinee's heart rate during the final 15 seconds of both the second and third minute of this stage. If

these two heart rates are not within 5 beats per minute of each other, have the examinee continue to pedal at this workload for an additional minute and record heart rate again. The workload will not be increased until the heart rate levels off to within 5 beats per minute for two consecutive minutes.

4) If the heart rates from the last two minutes of this stage are within 5 beats per minute of each other, increase the workload according to Table 2.5, and have the examinee complete another 3-minute stage.

5) Record the examinee's heart rate at the end of the second and third minute of this stage, again looking for two consecutive heart rates within 5 beats per minute of each other.

6) Continue to increase the workload and record heart rate until the examinee has completed two stages with heart rates between 110 and 150 beats per minute. If heart rate during the first stage is greater than 110 beats per minute, use this stage as one of the two needed.

7) At the end of the test, remove the workload and have the examinee cool-down by pedaling easily for 5 minutes.

Scoring: Use Datasheet #2

Scores for this test are converted to an estimate of VO2 max (ml/kg/min).

1) Obtain the Estimated Maximal Physical Working Capacity by plotting the two exercise heart rates that were between 110 and 150 beats per minute at their respective workloads on the datasheet as shown in Figure 2.3.

2) Draw a straight line connecting these two points and extend it up to the examinee's maximal heart rate (max HR = 220-age).

3) Draw a straight line down from the point at which the line intersects the maximal heart rate to determine the examinee's maximal workload.

To calculate estimated VO2 max:

1) Multiply the maximum workload (Watts) from the datasheet-plot by 12.

2) Multiply the examinee's bodyweight in Kg by 3.5.

3) Add the results of 1 and 2 above.

4) Divide the result by bodyweight in Kg.

5) Compare the estimated VO2 to Table 2.2.

Example:

30-year-old female, weighing 75 Kg, completes 3 stages of this test. Her results are below:

Workload 1 = 25 Watts   Average Exercise Heart Rate = 85

Workload 2 = 100 Watts   Average Exercise Heart Rate = 120

Workload 3 = 125 Watts   Average Exercise Heart Rate = 135

Plot heart rates versus workloads on the datasheet as shown in Figure 2.3.

Maximum workload from Figure 2.3 = 215 Watts.

1) *Multiply 215 Watts by 12*: 215 x 12 = 2580

2) *Multiply weight by 3.5*: 75 Kg x 3.5 = 262.5

3) *Add the results of 1 and 2 above*: 2580 + 262.5 = 2842.5

4) *Divide by weight in Kg*: 2842.5 / 75 = 37.9

5) *Compare to Table 2.2* = Average

COOPER 12-MINUTE RUN/WALK TEST

For additional information see references 15, 17, 30

Equipment: Stopwatch, Measured distance on a track or street.

Objective: To determine estimated VO2 max.

Procedure:

This test is best performed on a marked, ¼ mile, standard length track found at most public schools; or you can mark off distances in a neighborhood using the odometer in a car.

1) Determine a starting point.

2) Instruct the examinee that they should run, or run and walk as far as possible in 12 minutes.

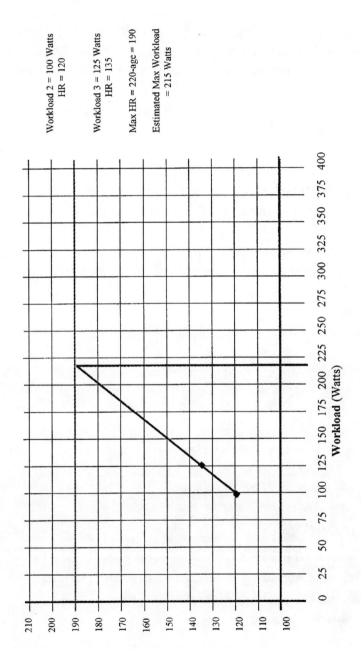

Figure 2.3—Example: YMCA Physical Working Capacity Test – Maximal workload extrapolation

3) Begin the test using the command "Ready, Go". Start the stopwatch when the examinee begins moving. The total distance covered is the score for this test, so motivate them to keep moving as fast as possible for the entire 12 minutes.

4) At the end of the 12-minutes, note the total distance covered, and have the examinee cool down by walking an additional 5 minutes.

Scoring: Use Datasheet #3
Scores for this test are converted to an estimate of VO2 max (ml/kg/min). The distance covered in miles must be in decimal form (i.e. 1 ½ miles = 1.50 miles).

To determine estimated VO2:

1) Multiply the distance covered in miles for the 12-minute run/walk by 35.9712

2) Subtract 11.2872.

3) Compare the estimated VO2 to table 2.2.

Estimated VO2 = *(Distance covered (miles) x 35.9712) – 11.2872*

Example:
A 27-year-old female covers 1.50 miles in the 12 minutes.
1) *1.50 miles x 35.9712 = 53.9568*
2) *53.9568—11.2872 =* 42.67 ml/kg/min
3) *Compare to Table 2.2* : Average

1.5-MILE RUN

For additional information see references 16, 27
Equipment: Stopwatch, Measured distance of 1.5 miles.
Objective: To determine estimated VO2 max.
Procedure:

This test is best performed on a marked, ¼ mile, standard length track found at most public schools; or mark off the distance in a neighborhood using the odometer in a car.

1) Instruct the examinee that they should run, or run and walk the 1.5-mile distance as fast as possible.

2) Begin the test using the command "Ready, Go". Start the stopwatch when the examinee begins moving.

3) Use the stopwatch to measure the amount of time it takes the examinee to complete the 1.5 miles.

4) Have the examinee cool down by walking approximately 5 minutes.

Scoring: Use Datasheet #4

The results of this test are not an estimate of maximal VO2, but a measure of the peak VO2 used during this test. You may compare the results of this test to Table 2.2 to obtain a score or use the test-retest method to compare changes over time.

1) Convert the elapsed time to decimal form by dividing any seconds by 60 (i.e. 8 min 20 seconds = 8 + 20/60 = 8.33 minutes).

2) Divide 2413.5 by the elapsed time.

3) Multiply by 0.2.

4) Add 3.5. The result is the estimated VO2 for this test.

Example:

A 35-year-old male completes the 1.5 miles in 14 minutes and 15 seconds

1) *Convert time to decimal form*: 14 minutes + 15/60 = 14.25 minutes.

2) *Divide 2413.5 by time*: 2413.5 / 14.25 = 169.37

3) *Multiply result by 0.2*: 169.37 x 0.2 = 33.87

4) *Add 3.5 to result*: 33.87 + 3.5 = 37.37

5) *Compare to Table 2.2* = Average

YOUTH DISTANCE RUN (modification of 1.5 Mile Run)

For additional information see references 16, 27, 37, 38
Equipment: Stopwatch, Measured distance of ½ and 1 mile.
Objective: To assess cardiovascular fitness.
Procedure:
This test is best performed on a marked, ¼ mile, standard length track found at most public schools; or mark off the distance in a neighborhood using the odometer in a car.

1) Instruct the examinee that they should run, or run and walk the ½ mile distance (6–7 year olds) or 1 mile distance (8-18 year olds) as fast as possible.

2) Begin the test using the command "Ready, Go". Start the stopwatch when the examinee begins moving.

3) Use the stopwatch to measure the amount of time it takes the examinee to complete the distance.

4) Have the examinee cool down by walking approximately 5 minutes.

Scoring: Use Datasheet #5
The score is the total time it takes to cover the ½ or 1 mile distance. Compare to Table 2.6.

Table 2.6

Scores for Youth Distance Run (minutes : seconds)

	Excellent	Good	Average	Fair	Low
Male					
6	< 4:27	4:27-4:52	4:53-5:58	5:59-6:40	> 6:40
7	< 4:11	4:11-4:33	4:34-5:35	5:36-6:20	> 6:20
8	< 8:46	8:46-9:29	9:30-12:14	12:15-14:05	>14:05
9	< 8:10	8:10-9:00	9:01-11:44	11:45-13:37	> 13:37
10	< 8:13	8:13-8:48	8:49-11:00	11:01-12:27	> 12:27
11	< 7:25	7:25-8:02	8:03-10:32	10:33-12:07	> 12:07
12	< 7:13	7:13-7:53	7:54-10:13	10:14-11:48	> 11:48
13	< 6:48	6:48-7:14	7:15-9:06	9:07-10:38	> 10:38
14	< 6:27	6:27-7:08	7:09-9:10	9:11-10:34	> 10:34
15	< 6:23	6:23-6:52	6:53-8:30	8:31-10:13	> 10:13
16	< 6:13	6:13-6:39	6:40-8:18	8:19-9:36	> 9:36
17	< 6:08	6:08-6:40	6:41-8:37	8:38-10:43	> 10:43
18	< 6:10	6:10-6:42	6:43-8:34	8:35-10:50	> 10:50
Female					
6	< 4:46	4:46-5:13	5:14-6:14	6:15-6:51	> 6:51
7	< 4:32	4:32-4:54	4:55-6:01	6:02-6:38	> 6:38
8	< 9:39	9:39-10:23	10:24-12:59	13:00-14:48	> 14:48
9	< 9:08	9:08-9:50	9:51-12:45	12:46-14:31	> 14:31
10	< 9:09	9:09-10:09	10:10-12:52	12:53-14:20	> 14:20
11	< 8:45	8:45-9:56	9:57-12:54	12:55-14:35	> 14:35
12	< 8:34	8:34-9:52	9:53-12:33	12:34-14:07	> 14:07
13	< 8:27	8:27-9:30	9:31-12:17	12:18-13:45	> 13:45
14	< 8:11	8:11-9:16	9:17-11:49	11:50-13:13	> 13:13
15	< 8:23	8:23-9:28	9:29-12:18	12:19-14:07	> 14:07
16	< 8:28	8:28-9:25	9:26-12:10	12:11-13:42	> 13:42
17	< 8:20	8:20-9:26	9:27-12:03	12:04-13:46	> 13:46
18	< 8:22	8:22-9:31	9:32-12:14	12:15-15:18	> 15:18

*Data from Ross et al. (1985,1987)

ROCKPORT WALK TEST

For additional information see references 4, 31, 39
Equipment: Stopwatch, Measured distance of 1 mile, Stethoscope.
Objective: To determine estimated VO2 max.

Procedure:
This test is best performed on a marked, ¼ mile, standard length track found at most public schools; or mark off the distance in a neighborhood using the odometer in a car.

1) Have the examinee warm-up by walking for 5 minutes.

2) Determine a starting position.

3) Encourage them to walk as fast as possible, but not to jog or run. Begin the test with the command "Ready, Go". Start the stopwatch when the examinee begins moving.

4) Measure the amount of time it takes to complete one mile.

5) At the end of one mile, immediately measure the examinee's heart rate for 15 seconds. Multiply the 15-second heart rate by 4 to obtain a final exercise heart rate.

6) Have them cool down by walking an additional 5 minutes.

Scoring: Use Datasheet #6
1) Convert the elapsed time to decimal form by dividing any seconds by 60 (i.e. 8 min 20 seconds = 8 + 20/60 = 8.33 minutes).

2) Use the equation below to determine the estimated VO2 max and compare to Table 2.2.

$$
\begin{aligned}
\text{VO2 max} = \quad & 132.853 \\
& - (0.0769 \text{ x weight in pounds}) \\
& - (0.3877 \text{ x age in years}) \\
& + (6.315 \text{ x gender: Male} = 1, \text{Female} = 2) \\
& - (3.2649 \text{ x time to complete mile}) \\
& - (0.1565 \text{ x final heart rate})
\end{aligned}
$$

Example:
A 55-year-old Male, weight 180 lbs., completed 1-mile in 15 minutes and 35 seconds. Final heart rate was 120 beats per minute.

1) Convert time to decimal form: 35/60 = 0.58 + 15 = 15.58

2) Calculate each step before final computation:

132.853 (Given amount)	=	132.853
- (0.0769 x 180 lbs)	=	-13.842
- (0.3877 x 55 years)	=	-21.324
+ (6.315 x 1) Male = 1	=	+ 6.315
- (3.2649 x 15.58)	=	-50.867
- (0.1565 x 120)	=	-18.78
		34.36

3) Compare to Table 2.2 for VO2: Average

HARVARD STEP TEST

For additional information see references 13, 17, 30

Equipment: Bench (20 inches high, 12 inches deep), Stopwatch, Metronome or audiotape with a prerecorded cadence (such as an aerobics music tape), Stethoscope

Objective: To determine estimated VO2 max.

Procedure:

Set the metronome at 120 beats per minute, or use a prerecorded tape with a cadence of 120 beats per minute. The stepping rate will be 30 steps per minute, performed by stepping to the rhythm of Up-Up-Down-Down, one movement per beat, as shown in Figure 2.4.

1) Have the examinee stand behind the step with hands on the waist.

2) Start the test on the command "Ready, Go". Start the stopwatch when the examinee begins the first step. This stepping rate is continued for 5 minutes or until the examinee cannot maintain the pace.

3) Record the total time completed in minutes and seconds.

4) Measure total number of heart beats during a 30-second period starting exactly 1 minute after the end of the test. This is not a measure of heart rate, but how many beats occur in this 30-second time period.

Scoring: Use Datasheet #7

The exercise time and heart rate are compared to Table 2.7. The score is an arbitrary number that can only be used for this test. Interpretation of the score is as follows:

Low = Below 50

Average = 50 - 80

Good = Above 80

Example:

An examinee completes 3 ½ minutes of stepping before losing cadence. The number of heart beats between 1 and 1 ½ minutes after exercise is 62. Compare to Table 2.7, score is 57 = Average.

Figure 2.4—Basic stepping rhythm: Up-Up-Down-Down. TOP LEFT: First step up. TOP RIGHT: Second step up, both legs completely straight. BOTTOM LEFT: First step down. BOTTOM RIGHT: Second step down, both feet on the floor.

Table 2.7

Scores for the Harvard Step Test

Minutes Completed	Total heart beats between 1 and 1 ½ minutes after exercise.											
	40-44	45-49	50-54	55-59	60-64	65-69	70-74	75-79	80-84	85-89	90-94	95-99
0 – ½	6	6	5	5	4	4	4	4	3	3	3	3
½—1	19	17	16	14	13	12	11	11	10	9	9	8
1 – 1½	32	29	26	24	22	20	19	18	17	16	15	14
1½—2	45	41	38	34	31	29	27	25	23	22	21	20
2 – 2½	58	52	47	43	40	36	34	32	30	28	27	25
2 ½—3	71	64	58	53	48	45	42	39	37	34	33	31
3 – 3 ½	84	75	68	62	57	53	49	46	43	41	39	37
3 ½—4	97	87	79	72	66	61	57	53	50	47	45	42
4 – 4 ½	110	98	89	82	75	75	60	61	57	54	51	48
4 ½—5	123	110	100	91	84	77	72	68	63	60	57	54
5	129	116	105	96	88	82	76	71	67	63	60	56

* Data from Brouha (1943)

QUEENS COLLEGE STEP TEST

For additional information see references 28, 42

Equipment: Bench (16-17 inches high, 12 inches deep), Metronome or prerecorded aerobics tape, Stopwatch, Stethoscope

Objective: To determine estimated VO2 max.

Procedure:

Set the metronome or use a prerecorded aerobics tape for a cadence of 22 steps/minute for women (88 beats per minute) or 24 steps/minute for men (96 beats per minute).

1) Start the test on the command "Ready, Go". Start the stopwatch when the examinee begins the first step. Have the examinee step for 3 minutes at the determined cadence according to the stepping procedure shown in Figure 2.4 (Up, Up, Down, Down).

2) At the end of 3 minutes, use the stethoscope to count heart rate for 15 seconds; and multiply by 4 to obtain beats per minute.

Scoring: Use Datasheet #8
Calculate estimated VO2 max using the appropriate calculation below. Compare to Table 2.2.

Men: Estimated VO2 max = 111.33 – (0.42 x Heart rate)

Women: Estimated VO2 Max = 65.81 – (0.185 x Heart rate)

Example:
A 38-year-old female completes the test with a final 15-second heart rate of 43.

1) Multiply 43 x 4 = 172 beats per minute

2) VO2 Max   = 65.81- (0.185 x 172)

                           = 65.81- 31.82

                           = 33.99

3) Compare to Table 2.2 = Average

Chapter 3:

Muscular Strength & Endurance Tests

Muscular strength and muscular endurance are two separate properties that are often grouped together for testing purposes. It is important to understand the difference between the two because they are quite unalike. Muscular strength, often referred to as a person's one rep max (1RM), is defined as the amount of weight a person can lift one time before volitional fatigue. Muscular endurance is the ability to lift a sub-maximal amount of weight a number of times before becoming fatigued. The tests in this section involve several different muscle groups so that the strength and endurance properties of the entire body can be evaluated. The tests also cover two different types of muscular endurance testing; defined as absolute endurance and relative endurance.

Absolute endurance tests involve measuring the total number of repetitions each participant can do using the same weight. Examinees can be compared to each other, and claims of one having more endurance than another are valid. The YMCA Bench Press Test is an example of absolute muscular endurance.

Relative endurance tests use only the subject's body weight as resistance; therefore each subject will be working with a different amount of weight. The Pull-Up and Push-Ups Tests are examples of relative endurance. The Dynamic Muscular Endurance Test Battery is also a test of relative strength except that a percentage of each person's body weight is used as the resistance for each test. The result of each of these tests is the amount of work that a person can do relative to their body weight. These tests allow persons of different body weights to be measured on the same scale. Clients or athletes completing these tests can compare scores and claims of one having more endurance than another are valid relative to body weight.

The one rep max (1RM) tests are measurements of an individual's muscular strength. These tests require several warm-up sets prior to the attempt in order to prepare the muscle for maximal contraction and reduce the incidence of injury. One rep max tests are the most dangerous because they involve the client or athlete attempting to lift as much weight as possible one time.

With all of these tests, and 1RM tests especially, proper technique is crucial. Allowing a client or athlete to attempt additional repetitions after proper form is lost, or attempt a 1RM that you believe is beyond their ability is not recommended and may possibly injure the person. Use proper spotting techniques to insure the safety of your clients and athletes.

YMCA BENCH PRESS TEST

For additional information see references 11, 20

Equipment: 35 lb. barbell for females, 80 lb. barbell for males, Metronome, Weight training bench

Objective: To test the strength and endurance of the upper body (pectorals, deltoids and triceps muscles).

Procedure:

1) Set the metronome at 60 beats per minute. Each repetition must be done in cadence with the metronome by executing an up movement with one beat, and a down movement with the next beat, for a cadence of 30 full repetitions per minute.

2) The examinee assumes a supine (lying) position on the bench with the knees bent to 90 degrees and feet flat on the floor; grasping the barbell with hands shoulder width apart.

3) The test begins with the weight in the "Down" position just above the chest. To complete one repetition, the weight must be pressed upward until the elbows are fully extended ("Up" position), and then lowered to the starting position (Figure 3.1).

4) The test is terminated when the examinee is unable to fully extend the elbows during the up movement, or is unable to maintain cadence.

Scoring: Use Datasheet #9

The score is the number of correctly performed repetitions. Compare to Table 3.1.

Table 3.1

Scores for YMCA Bench Press Test

Age	Excellent	Good	Average	Fair	Low
Male:					
18-25	>41	30-41	22-29	13-21	0-12
26-35	>39	26-39	20-25	12-19	0-11
36-45	>33	24-33	17-23	10-16	0-9
46-55	>27	20-27	12-19	6-11	0-5
56-65	>23	14-23	8-13	4-7	0-3
66+	>19	10-19	6-9	2-5	0-1
Female:					
18-25	>41	28-41	20-27	12-19	0-11
26-35	>40	25-39	17-24	9-16	0-8
36-45	>32	21-31	13-20	8-12	0-7
46-55	>29	20-29	11-19	5-10	0-4
56-65	>29	16-29	9-15	3-8	0-2
66+	>21	12-21	6-11	2-5	0-1

*Data from Golding (1989)

Figure 3.1—YMCA Bench Press Test positions: TOP—Starting "Down" position. Bar just above but not touching the chest. BOTTOM—"Up" position. Arms completely straight, elbows extended with bar balanced above chest.

ISOMETRIC LEG SQUAT (WALL SIT) TEST

For additional information see references 14, 25

Equipment: Stopwatch, Wall

Objective: To test the static strength and endurance of the lower body (Quadriceps muscles).

Procedure:

1) The examinee assumes a sitting position against a solid wall without the aid of a chair (Figure 3.2). The knees are bent at 90 degrees so that the thighs are parallel to the floor and the lower legs are perpendicular to the floor. The feet are flat on the floor, pointed straight ahead and hip width apart. The head, shoulders and lower back should remain in contact with the wall at all times.

2) Once the examinee is in position, start the stopwatch.

3) The test is terminated when the examinee can no longer maintain the position.

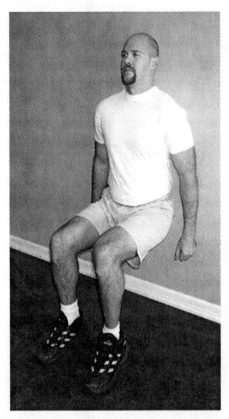

Figure 3.2—Isometric Leg Squat (Wall Sit) position. Subject assumes a seated position against a wall. Keep the head, shoulders and lower back in contact with the wall, feet flat on floor, pointed straight ahead and hip width apart. Knees bent 90 degrees, thighs parallel to floor, lower legs perpendicular to the floor.

Scoring: Use Datasheet #10

The score is the amount of time the position is maintained (Minutes / Seconds). The score on this test can be used for future reference when retesting to measure change. No norms are provided.

PULL-UP TEST

For additional information see references 3, 27

Equipment: A horizontal bar (pull-up bar) at least 6 inches taller than the examinee when their arms and hands are stretched out over their head.

Objective: To test the strength and endurance of the upper body (Latissimus dorsi (lats) and biceps muscles).

Procedure:

1) The examinee grips the horizontal bar, hands approximately shoulder width apart, using a pronated grip (palms facing away from the body) or a supinated grip (palms facing toward the body) (Figure 3.3).

2) Starting in the outstretched position, pull upward until the chin is above the level of the bar (Figure 3.4) and return to the starting position. This sequence equals one repetition. The legs should remain straight during the movement, and the body should not swing. If body swing does occur, the tester may place an arm across the front of the examinee's thighs to stop any swinging movement.

3) Repeat step 2 until examinee cannot complete the repetition.

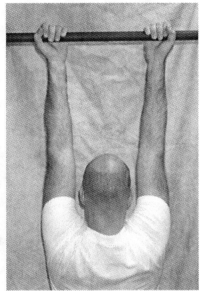

Figure 3.3—Handgrip positions for Pull-Up Test. LEFT—Pronated "overhand" grip. RIGHT—Supinated "underhand" grip.

Scoring: Use Datasheet #11

The score is the number of correct repetitions performed. Compare the score to Table 3.2.

Table 3.2				
Scores for Pull-Up Test				
Excellent	**Good**	**Average**	**Fair**	**Low**
>14	11-14	7-10	4-6	0-3

*Data from Johnson & Nelson (1986)

Figure 3.4—Finish position for Pull-up Test. Subject's chin is above the level of the bar.

SIT-UPS TEST

For additional information see references 11, 20, 27, 45

Equipment: Padded floor mat, Stopwatch

Objective: To test the strength and endurance of the abdominal and hip flexor muscles.

Procedure:

1) Determine the correct angle of knee flexion by having the examinee sit on the mat with feet flat, knees bent, and the back straight. Place the hands on the shoulders and touch the elbows to the knees while the back is perpendicular to the floor (Figure 3.5).

2) The examinee lies back to the floor while keeping the hands on the shoulders. An assistant may hold the feet firmly in place.

3) Give the command "Ready, Go". Start the stopwatch when the examinee begins moving. The examinee flexes the trunk and rolls the torso up until the elbows touch the knees (Figure 3.5), then returns to the mat with the head not touching.

4) Repeat repetitions as many times as possible in one minute. Partial repetitions do not count.

Scoring: Use Datasheet #12

The score is the number of complete sit-ups done in one minute. Compare to Table 3.3 (Youth) or Table 3.4 (Adult).

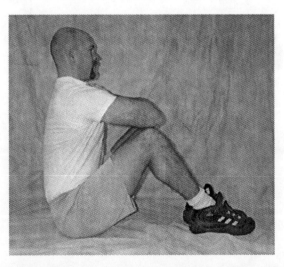

Figure 3.5—Proper knee flexion for Sit-Ups Test. Touch the elbows to the top of the knees while the feet are flat (can be held in place by an assistant), knees bent, back straight, and arms crossed with hands on the shoulders.

Table 3.3					
		Scores for Sit-Ups Test—Youth			
Age:	**Low**	**Fair**	**Average**	**Good**	**Excellent**
Male:					
6	< 9	9-14	15-24	25-28	> 28
7	< 12	12-18	19-28	29-32	> 32
8	< 15	15-20	21-30	31-35	> 35
9	< 16	16-23	24-33	34-39	> 39
10	< 22	22-28	29-40	41-47	> 47
11	< 22	22-30	31-41	42-48	> 48
12	< 25	25-32	33-44	45-50	> 50
13	< 28	28-32	33-46	47-52	> 52
14	< 30	30-35	36-47	48-52	> 52
15	< 31	31-36	37-48	49-53	> 53
16	< 32	32-38	39-49	50-55	> 55
17	< 31	31-37	38-50	51-56	> 56
Female:					
6	< 6	6-14	15-23	24-28	> 28
7	< 11	11-16	17-27	28-33	> 33
8	< 13	13-19	20-29	30-34	> 34
9	< 15	15-21	22-31	32-36	> 36
10	< 20	20-25	26-37	38-43	> 43
11	< 20	20-26	27-37	38-42	> 42
12	< 21	21-28	29-40	41-46	> 46
13	< 21	21-27	28-40	41-46	> 46
14	< 23	23-29	30-41	42-47	> 47
15	< 24	24-30	31-40	41-45	> 45
16	< 23	23-30	31-40	41-49	> 49
17	< 24	24-30	31-40	41-47	> 47

*Data from Ross et al. (1985,1987)

Table 3.4 Scores for Sit-Ups Test—Adult							
Age:	**Excellent**	**Good**	**Above Average**	**Average**	**Below Average**	**Fair**	**Low**
Males							
18-25	>48	44-48	39-43	35-38	31-34	25-30	0-24
26-35	>45	40-45	35-39	31-34	28-30	23-27	0-22
36-45	>41	35-41	30-34	27-29	23-26	17-22	0-16
46-55	>35	29-35	25-28	22-24	18-21	13-17	0-12
56-65	>31	25-31	21-24	17-20	13-16	9-12	0-8
66+	>28	22-28	19-21	15-18	11-14	7-10	0-6
Females							
18-25	>43	37-43	33-36	29-32	25-28	19-24	0-18
26-35	>39	33-39	29-32	25-28	21-24	15-20	0-14
36-45	>32	27-32	23-26	19-22	15-18	8-14	0-8
46-55	>27	22-27	18-21	14-17	10-13	5-9	0-4
56-65	>23	18-23	13-17	10-12	7-9	3-6	0-2
66+	>23	17-23	14-16	11-13	5-10	2-4	0-1

*Data from Baumgartner & Jackson (1987)

PUSH-UP TEST

For additional information see reference 34, 40, 41

Equipment: Mat (optional)

Objective: To assess upper body strength and endurance (pectorals, deltoid, and triceps muscles).

Procedure:

Males perform this test in the traditional push-up technique. Females may use either the traditional or the modified technique. Females using the traditional technique may be scored with the Male category.

1) Have the examinee assume the correct starting position for the technique they will be using (traditional or modified) as shown in Figure 3.6. The starting position begins with the hands on the floor,

slightly wider than shoulder width, and either the knees (modified) or toes (traditional) touching the floor. The body should be kept straight and rigid.

2) Start in the "Up" position (Figure 3.6).

3) The examinee should lower the body until the elbows and the shoulders are at the same height (upper arm parallel to the floor), then return to the "Up" position. This counts as one repetition.

4) Continue repetitions until examinee is unable to complete a correct repetition. Incorrect repetitions occur if the body is not kept rigid, and are disqualified.

Scoring: Use Datasheet #13

Record the number of correctly performed pushups. Compare to Table 3.5 (Youth) or Table 3.6 (Adult).

Table 3.5

Scores for Push-Up Test—Youth (number completed)

	Low	Fair	Average	Good	Excellent
Male:					
6	< 1	1-3	4-10	11-15	> 15
7	< 1	1-4	5-13	14-19	> 19
8	< 3	3-6	7-14	15-20	> 20
9	< 3	3-6	7-15	16-20	> 20
10	0	0	0-4	5-8	> 8
11	0	0	0-5	6-8	> 8
12	0	0	0-5	6-8	> 8
13	0	0-1	2-7	8-10	> 10
14	0	0-2	3-8	9-12	> 12
15	< 1	1-4	5-10	11-14	> 14
16	< 2	2-6	7-12	13-14	> 14
17	< 2	2-5	6-12	13-15	> 15
18	< 3	3-6	7-13	14-16	> 16
Female:					
6	0	0	0-1	2	> 2
7	0	0-3	4-9	10-13	> 13
8	< 1	1-4	5-11	12-16	> 16
9	< 1	1-4	5-11	12-17	> 17
10	0	0	0-4	5-8	> 8
11	0	0	0-5	6-8	> 8
12	0	0	0-5	6-8	> 8
13	0	0-1	2-7	8-10	> 10
14	0	0-2	3-8	9-12	> 12
15	< 1	1-4	5-10	11-14	> 14
16	< 2	2-6	7-12	13-14	> 14
17	< 2	2-5	6-12	13-15	> 15
18	< 3	3-6	7-13	14-16	> 16

*Data from Ross et al. (1985, 1987)

Table 3.6

Scores for Push-Up Test—Adult (number completed)

	Excellent	Good	Average	Fair	Low
Male					
20-29	>35	29-35	22-28	17-21	<17
30-39	>29	22-29	17-21	12-16	<12
40-49	>21	17-21	13-16	10-12	<10
50-59	>20	13-20	10-12	7-9	<7
60-69	>17	11-17	8-10	5-7	<5
Female					
20-29	>29	21-29	15-20	10-14	<10
30-39	>26	20-26	13-19	8-12	<8
40-49	>23	15-23	11-14	5-10	<5
50-59	>20	11-20	7-10	2-6	<2
60-69	>16	12-16	5-11	1-4	<1

*Data from Morrow (2000)

Figure 3.6—Push-Up positions. TOP: Modified. BOTTOM: Traditional

DYNAMIC MUSCULAR ENDURANCE TEST BATTERY

For additional information see reference 23

Procedure Note:

This is a battery of tests that involve each of the major muscle groups. In order to obtain a score, the examinee must complete all seven tests. The tests can be performed in any order, with rest in between, but should be performed on the same day. The weight used in each test is a percentage of the examinee's body weight in pounds.

Scoring: Use Datasheet #14

Compile test scores and compute an overall score by adding up the total number of repetitions for each test (maximum of 15 per test). Compare overall score to Table 3.7.

Table 3.7		
Scores for Dynamic Muscular Endurance Test		
	Total repetitions	**Rating**
	91 – 105	Excellent
	77 – 90	Very Good
	63 – 76	Good
	49 – 62	Average
	35 – 48	Fair
	< 35	Low
*Data from Heyward (1998)		

TEST #1: Arm Curl

Equipment: Barbell and free-weights.

Percent of body weight to be lifted: Men = 33% (0.33)   Women = 25% (0.25)

Objective: To test the strength and endurance of the biceps muscles.

Procedure:

1) Determine the weight to be used by multiplying the individual's weight in pounds by the percentage shown above, and record on Datasheet #14.

2) The examinee should stand against a wall so that the head and buttocks touch the wall, and the feet approximately 1 foot away from the wall (Figure 3.7).

3) Begin with the arms outstretched and the weight in the "down" position; keep the elbows at the sides and "curl" the weight up to the shoulders ("up" position), and return to the down position. This counts as one repetition.

4) Complete as many repetitions as possible. Failure to raise the barbell to the shoulders, swinging the elbows from the sides, or either the head or buttocks moving away from the wall disqualifies a repetition.

5) Record the number of completed repetitions (maximum of 15) on Datasheet #14.

Figure 3.7—Arm Curl positions. Head and buttocks touching the wall and feet about 1 foot away from the wall. LEFT—Start "Down" position, arms fully extended. RIGHT—Finish "Up" position, elbows bent and hands up to the shoulders

TEST #2: Bench Press

Equipment: Barbell and free-weights, Weight bench

Percentage of body-weight to be lifted: Men = 66% (0.66)   Women = 50% (0.50)

Objective: To test the strength and endurance of the pectorals, deltoids and triceps muscles.

Procedure:

1) Determine the weight to be used by multiplying the individual's weight in pounds by the percentage shown above, and record on Datasheet #14.

2) The examinee assumes a supine (lying) position on the bench with the knees bent at 90 degrees and feet flat on the floor, grasping the barbell with hands shoulder width apart.

3) The test begins with the weight in the down position just above the chest. To complete one repetition, the weight must be pressed upward until the elbows are fully extended, and then lowered to the starting position (Figure 3.1).

4) Complete as many repetitions as possible. Failure to fully extend the elbows, or lower the barbell completely down to the chest disqualifies the repetition.

5) Record the number of completed repetitions (maximum of 15) on Datasheet #14.

TEST #3: Lat Pull-down

Equipment: Lat Pull-down machine

Percentage of body-weight to be lifted: Men = 66% (0.66) Women = 50% (0.50)

Objective: To test the strength and endurance of the Latissimus dorsi and biceps muscles.

Procedure:

1) Determine the weight to be used by multiplying the individual's weight in pounds by the percentage shown above, and record on Datasheet #14.

2) Have the examinee sit facing the machine and grasp the bar with a pronated (overhand) grip; hands approximately shoulder width apart (Figure 3.8).

3) Starting in the outstretched "up" position, pull the bar down in front of the head until the hands are at the same level as the shoulders (Figure 3.8), and return to the up position. This counts as one repetition.

4) Complete as many repetitions as possible. Failure to bring the bar down to the shoulders or return the bar to the fully outstretched position disqualifies the repetition.

5) Record the number of completed repetitions (maximum of 15) on Datasheet #14.

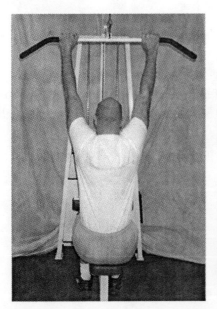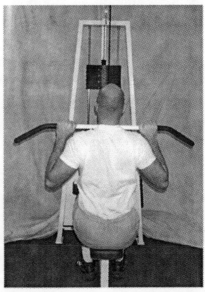

Figure 3.8—Lat Pulldown positions. LEFT: Start "Up" position, arms completely extended. RIGHT: Finish position, hands at the same level as the shoulders.

TEST #4: Triceps extension

Equipment: Lat pull-down machine or High-cable pulley machine

Percentage of body-weight to be lifted: Men = 33% (0.33) Women = 33% (0.33)

Objective: To test the strength and endurance of the triceps muscles.

Procedure:

1) Determine the weight to be used by multiplying the individual's weight in pounds by the percentage shown above, and record on Datasheet #14.

2) The examinee should stand slightly behind the cable, elbows at the sides, using a pronated (overhand) grip approximately as wide as the shoulders (Figure 3.9).

3) Beginning in the "up" position, press the weight down until the arms are fully extended (Figure 3.9), and return to the up position. This counts as one repetition.

4) Complete as many repetitions as possible. Failure to fully extend the arms, bring the weight completely back up to the starting position, moving the elbows from the sides, or leaning over the weight disqualifies the repetition.

5) Record the number of completed repetitions (maximum of 15) on Datasheet #14.

 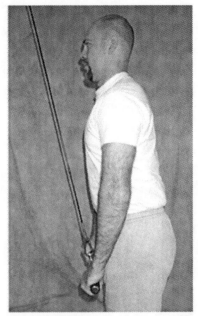

Figure 3.9—Triceps Extension positions. LEFT: Start "Up" position. Elbows at the sides and bent so that hands and shoulders are approximately at the same level. RIGHT: Finish. Arms are fully extended.

TEST #5: Leg extension

Equipment: Leg extension machine

Percentage of body-weight to be lifted: Men = 50% (0.50) Women = 50% (0.50)

Objective: To test the strength and endurance of the quadriceps muscles.

Procedure:

1) Determine the weight to be used by multiplying the individual's weight in pounds by the percentage shown above, and record on Datasheet #14.

2) The examinee should sit upright in the machine far enough back so that the knees are in alignment with the pivotal axis of the machine (this will vary between machines).

3) Fully extending the legs, then returning them to the bottom position counts as one repetition (Figure 3.10).

4) Complete as many repetitions as possible. Failure to fully extend the legs or return them completely to the bottom position disqualifies the repetition.

5) Record the number of completed repetitions (maximum of 15) on Datasheet #14.

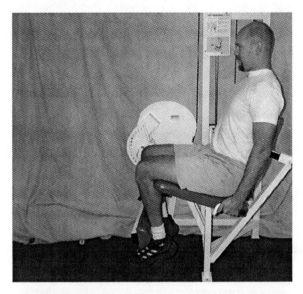

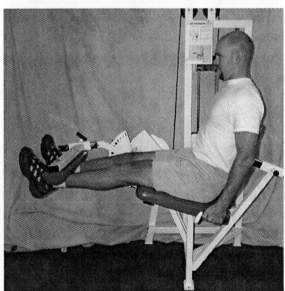

Figure 3.10—Leg Extension positions. TOP: Start. Knees bent and weight in down position. BOTTOM: Finish. Legs fully extended.

TEST #6: Leg curl
   Equipment: Lying or seated leg curl machine
   Percentage of body-weight to be lifted: Men = 33% (0.33)
Women = 33% (0.33)
   Objective: To test the strength and endurance of the hamstring muscles.
   Procedure:
   1) Determine the weight to be used by multiplying the individual's weight in pounds by the percentage shown above, and record on Datasheet #14.
   2) The examinee should be situated in the machine so that the knees are in alignment with the pivotal axis of the machine, and the leg pad placed just above the ankle.
   3) Moving the legs from fully extended to approximately 90 degrees flexion (Figure 3.11 & 3.12), then back down counts as one repetition.
   4) Complete as many repetitions as possible. Failure to fully extend the legs at the end of each repetition, or to reach 90 degrees of flexion disqualifies the repetition.
   5) Record the number of completed repetitions (maximum of 15) on Datasheet #14.

TEST #7: Bent-knee sit up
   Equipment: Exercise mat
   Objective: To test the strength and endurance of the abdominal and hip flexor muscles.
   Procedure:
   1) Determine the correct angle of knee flexion by having the examinee sit on the mat with feet flat, knees bent, and the back straight. Place the hands on the shoulders and touch the elbows to the knees while the back is perpendicular to the floor (Figure 3.5).
   2) The examinee lies back to the floor while keeping the hands on the shoulders, and with an assistant holding the feet firmly in place.

3) On command, the examinee flexes the trunk and rolls the torso up until the elbows touch the knees (Figure 3.5) and returns to the mat with the head not touching.

4) Complete as many repetitions as possible. Failure to touch the elbows to the knees, or not returning completely to the mat disqualifies the repetition.

5) Record the number of completed repetitions (maximum of 15) on Datasheet #14.

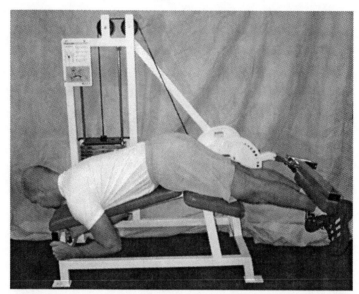

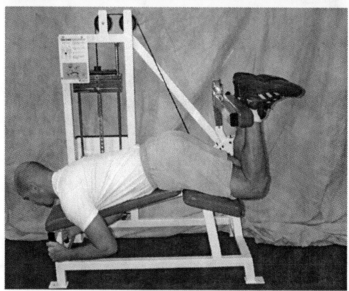

Figure 3.11—Lying Leg Curl positions. TOP: Start. Legs fully extended. BOTTOM: Finish. Legs bent approximately 90 degrees.

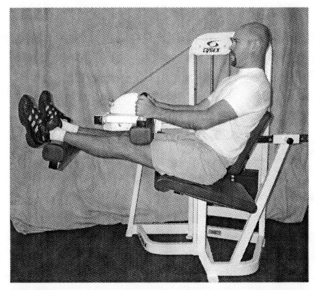

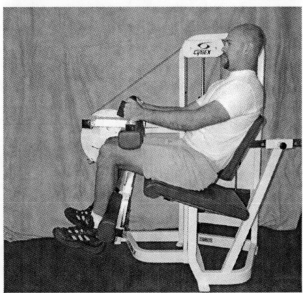

Figure 3.12—Seated Leg Curl positions. TOP: Start. Legs fully extended. BOTTOM: Finish. Legs bent approximately 90 degrees.

ONE REP MAX TESTS (1RM)

A one rep max (1RM) test can be performed for any exercise or for any muscle group. Proper form and spotters must be used when performing 1RM tests. Two procedures for determining 1RM are available and either can be used with any muscle group or exercise.

Procedure #1:

1) Have the examinee complete a warm-up set using a weight that allows 7-10 repetitions.

2) Allow 1-2 minutes of rest.

3) Increase the weight for a set that allows 3-6 repetitions.

4) Allow 2-3 minutes of rest.

5) Increase the weight for a set that allows 2-3 repetitions.

6) Allow 3-4 minutes of rest.

7) Increase the load 10-20 pounds for upper body exercises, or 30-40 pounds for lower body exercises. Have the examinee attempt a 1RM.

8) If they are successful, increase the weight by 5 pounds for upper body exercises, or 10 pounds for lower body exercises, and have them attempt another 1RM after 3-4 minutes of rest. If they were unsuccessful, decrease the weight by 5 pounds for upper body exercises, or 10 pounds for lower body exercises, and have them attempt another 1RM after 3-4 minutes of rest.

9) Repeat step 8 until a 1RM is established. Several attempts may have to be made. If the examinee becomes fatigued, allow further rest between sets.

Procedure #2:

1) Determine a weight with which the examinee can complete a ten rep max (10RM). A 10RM is a weight that can be lifted no more than 10 times.

2) Divide this weight by 0.67 to determine the estimated 1RM.

3) After 3-4 minutes rest, have the examinee attempt a 1RM with the calculated weight.

4) If they are successful, increase the weight by 5 pounds for upper body exercises, or 10 pounds for lower body exercises, and have them attempt another 1RM after 3-4 minutes of rest. If they were unsuccessful, decrease the weight by 5 pounds for upper body exercises, or 10 pounds for lower body exercises, and have the examinee attempt another 1RM after 3-4 minutes of rest.

5) Repeat step 4 until a 1RM is established. Several attempts may have to be made. If the examinee becomes fatigued, allow further rest between sets.

Scoring: Use Datasheet #15

One-repetition maximums (1RM) are not scored against norms. Test-retest data can provide measurement of changes resulting from the training program. Do not test 1RM repeatedly within a training program, but rather set a specific date approximately 3 months from the beginning of a training program to retest.

Chapter 4:

Power Tests

Tests of muscular power are tests of how quickly the body can exert force. These tests involve a single repetition performed as quickly and powerfully as possible. The definition of power is force divided by time $(p = f/t)$. The goal of power is to move the object as fast as possible. Strength training for power typically involves the clean-and-jerk and snatch exercises, plyometrics such as jumps or bounds, and medicine ball exercises. These exercises require the use of a large amount of muscle in a very short period of time. The ability of the muscle to contract "explosively" and produce force is the essence of power.

A person with more muscular strength will typically have more power than someone with less muscular strength. Sometimes that is not so. You may find that some clients have the ability to produce larger amounts of power compared to someone who is stronger than them. This is possible because power involves both strength and speed of execution. Training for power often necessitates training for better and faster execution, rather than increasing strength.

The exercises in this section involve moving either the body (vertical and standing long jumps) or a medicine ball (medicine ball put) as far as possible, as quickly as possible. The amount of muscle, and the specific muscle groups involved differs with each test. The Medicine Ball Put test involves only the muscles of the arms, shoulders, and chest. The

Standing Long Jump and Vertical Jump tests involve mainly the muscles of the legs, and secondarily the muscles of the upper body and trunk.

MEDICINE BALL PUT TEST

For additional information see references 27, 42

Equipment: 2.72 kilogram (6 lb.) medicine ball, Chair, Tape measure

Objective: To test the explosive power of the chest and arms (pectorals, deltoids, triceps).

Procedure:

1) Have the examinee sit in the chair with their back straight against the back of the chair. If the examinee sits or leans forward causing their back to move from the chair, the test is invalid.

2) The examinee grasps the ball, with one hand on each side of the ball, against the chest just under the chin (Figure 4.1). When ready, the examinee forcefully pushes the ball forward and upward attempting to put the ball as far away as possible.

3) Measure the distance from the front leg of the chair to spot where the ball lands, and record.

4) Repeat steps 2 and 3 for a total of 3 trials.

Figure 4.1—Medicine Ball Put Test position. Sit up straight in a chair, feet flat on the floor. Hold the ball at chest height, just under the chin.

Scoring: Use Datasheet #16

The score is the best of three trials, measured to the nearest foot. Compare to Table 4.1.

Table 4.1			
	Scores for Medicine Ball Put Test (feet)		
		Male	Female
Excellent		>25	>15
Good		21-25	13-14
Average		14-20	8-12
Fair		10-13	5-7
Low		0-9	0-4

*Data from Johnson & Nelson (1986)

STANDING LONG JUMP TEST

For additional information see references 2, 11, 27

Equipment: Marking tape, Tape measure

Objective: Test the dynamic power generation of the lower body musculature in a horizontal movement.

Procedure:

1) Lay the tape measure out on the floor and place a line on the floor using the marking tape to serve as the starting line as shown in Figure 4.2.

2) The examinee should straddle the tape measure, with feet parallel, about shoulder width apart, and toes behind the starting line.

3) From the starting position, the examinee should squat and then jump horizontally as far as possible and land with their feet straddling the tape measure.

4) Measure the distance from the starting line to the tip of the examinee's toes at the landing point.

5) Repeat steps 2-4. Allow 3 trials.

Figure 4.2—Starting position for Standing Long Jump Test. Toes behind the starting line, feet straddling the center line.

Scoring: Use Datasheet #17

The score is the distance from the starting line to the tip of the examinee's toes at the landing point, measured to the nearest inch. If the examinee lands and takes a step, that jump must be repeated. Compare the longest distance to Table 4.2.

Table 4.2		
Scores for Standing Long Jump Test (feet & inches)		
	Male	**Female**
Excellent	>8'3"	>6'4"
Good	7'9"—8'3"	5'10"—6'4"
Average	6'11"—7'8"	4'11"—5'9"
Fair	6'1"—6'10"	4'4"—4'10"
Low	0—6'0"	0—4'3"

*Data from Johnson & Nelson (1986)

VERTICAL JUMP TEST

For additional information see references 27, 43, 46

Equipment: Chalk, Tape measure, Masking tape

Objective: Test the dynamic power generation of the lower body musculature in a vertical movement.

Procedure:

1) Place a strip of masking tape vertically on a wall. The examinee should stand with their dominant side against the wall, dominant arm stretched out over their head, and place a chalk mark on the masking tape at the highest point they can reach (Figure 4.3). This is the starting mark.

2) Rub the fingers of the examinee's dominant hand with chalk.

3) The examinee now squats and jumps as high as possible and makes another chalk mark on the masking tape as high as they can reach. The examinee can swing the arms, but is not allowed to run up to the jump or move their feet in any way.

4) Repeat steps 2 and 3. Allow three trials.

Figure 4.3—Vertical Jump set-up and marking. LEFT: Make a chalk mark on the tape to indicate the starting position by standing against the wall with the dominant arm outstretched. RIGHT: Without moving the feet, squat, jump as high as possible and make another mark on the tape.

Scoring: Use Datasheet #18

The score (measured in inches) is the distance between the start mark and the highest mark made. Compare to Table 4.3.

Table 4.3

Scores for Vertical Jump Test (inches)

	Male	Female
Excellent	>24	>13
Good	20—24	11 – 13
Average	14—19	7 – 10
Fair	9—13	3 – 6
Low	0—8	0 – 2

*Data from USVA (1967)

Chapter 5:

Speed Tests

Tests of speed involve covering a specified distance as fast as possible (50 yard dash), or covering as much distance as possible in a given amount of time (4 & 6 second dash). Speed is a function of how fast a person is able to move their body through space. These tests mainly involve the muscles of the lower body that propel the person, and the muscles of the upper body and trunk that provide support and opposing movements (arm action). Therefore the entire body is involved in these tests. Training for speed and improving scores will include not only muscular strength, but efficiency of running as well. Quite often, how a person runs can mean the difference between a low or excellent score.

To score well on a test of speed, a client or athlete must be able to run. The tests can be performed by walking if the examinee is not able to run; but the normative data is based on running and will not apply if the examinee walks. Test-retest measures can be used in this case.

4-SECOND AND 6-SECOND DASH

For additional information see reference 27

Equipment: Stopwatch, Whistle, Measured distance (track or football field is preferred).

Objective: To measure the amount of work that can be done (distance covered) in a specific time.

Procedure:

Mark off a clear, straight, level course every yard using some sort of marking device such as flags, poles in the ground, or colored tape.

1) The examinee stands behind the starting line. Give the signal "Ready, Go". Start the stopwatch when the examinee starts running.

2) At the end of the 4 or 6-second time, blow the whistle to signal the end of the test, and note the location of the examinee at the instant the whistle blew.

3) Record the distance covered on Datasheet #19.

4) Allow 3 trials with a few minutes of rest in between.

Scoring: Use Datasheet #19

The score is the farthest distance covered in the allowed time, measured to the nearest foot. Compare to Table 5.1 for 4-second dash, or Table 5.2 for 6-second dash.

Table 5.1

Scores for 4-second Dash (feet)

	Men	Women
Excellent	>93	>76
Good	88 – 92	72 – 75
Average	82 – 87	65 – 71
Fair	70 – 81	59 – 64
Low	0 – 69	0 – 58

*Data from Johnson & Nelson (1986)

Table 5.2

Scores for 6-Second Dash (feet)

	Men	Women
Excellent	>162	>135
Good	153 – 162	126 – 135
Average	126 – 152	105 – 125
Fair	111 – 125	87 – 104
Low	0 – 110	0 – 86

*Data from Johnson & Nelson (1986)

50-YARD DASH

For additional information see references 1, 32

Equipment: Stopwatch, Measured distance of 50 yards (150 feet).

Objective: To measure the time is takes to cover 50 yards.

Procedure:

1) Have the examinee stand at the designated starting point.

2) Give the command "Ready, Go". Start the stopwatch when the examinee begins moving, and stop it when they cross the finish line.

3) Record the elapsed time to the nearest tenth of a second.

4) Allow 3 trials, with 5-10 minutes rest in between.

Scoring: Use Datasheet #20

The score is the time it takes to cover 50 yards, measured to the tenth of a second. Compare the best of 3 trials to Table 5.3.

Table 5.3					
Scores for 50-Yard Dash (seconds)					
	Excellent	**Good**	**Average**	**Fair**	**Low**
Men	< 6.1	6.1 – 6.9	7.0 – 7.5	7.6 – 8.0	> 8.0
Women	< 6.4	6.4 – 7.6	7.7 – 8.0	8.1 – 8.5	> 8.5
Data from Matthews (1978)					

Chapter 6:

Flexibility Tests

Flexibility is defined as the range of motion available in a joint or group of joints, the capacity of a joint to move fluidly through its full range of motion, and as the ability of a person to move a part or parts of the body in a wide range of purposeful movements at the required speed. Which part of this definition you subscribe to depends on your application of flexibility. Flexibility is improved through a regular regimen of stretching. These tests of flexibility involve static stretches. That is, the tests require the examinee to stretch and hold a position without using momentum to gain the position, or bouncing to increase the stretch.

Prior to performing these tests, the examinee should be well warmed up, preferably with general cardiovascular exercise that will increase blood flow to the areas to be stretched. Never perform these tests without warming up, as that can cause damage to the muscle and tendon tissues.

MODIFIED SIT AND REACH TEST

For additional information see references 23, 27, 30, 40, 41

Equipment: Yardstick, Masking tape

Objective: To measure the flexibility of the lower back and hamstring muscles.

Procedure:

Place the yardstick against a wall with the zero-end away from the wall. Tape both ends in place, and make a mark across the 15-inch line.

1) The examinee sits on the floor and straddles the yardstick with the heels no further than 5 inches apart and placed even with the 15-inch mark (Figure 6.1).

2) When ready, the examinee places one hand on top of the other and reaches as far down the yardstick as possible (Figure 6.1). While reaching out, the heels must not move beyond the 15-inch mark, and the knees must remain straight and locked. It may be necessary to have assistants hold the knees down during the test.

3) Record the greatest distance reached to the nearest ¼ inch. Allow 3 trials.

Scoring: Use Datasheet #21

The score is the greatest distance reached during the best of three trials, measured to the nearest ¼ inch. Compare to Table 6.1.

Table 6.1					
Scores for Modified Sit and Reach Test (inches)					
Age	Excellent	Good	Average	Fair	Low
Male:					
6	> 16.0	15.5—16.0	12.5—15.0	10.5—12.0	< 10.5
7	> 16.0	15.5—16.0	12.0—15.0	10.0—11.5	< 10.0
8	> 16.0	15.0—16.0	12.0—14.5	9.5—11.5	< 9.5
9	> 15.5	15.0—15.5	11.5—14.5	9.5—11.0	< 9.5
10	> 16.0	15.0—16.0	12.0—14.5	10.0—11.5	< 10.0
11	> 16.5	15.5—16.5	12.0—15.0	9.5—11.5	< 9.5
12	> 16.0	15.5—16.0	11.5—15.0	8.5—11.0	< 8.5
13	> 16.5	15.5—16.5	11.5—15.0	9.0—11.0	< 9.0
14	> 17.5	16.0—17.5	11.5—15.5	9.0—11.0	< 9.0
15	> 18.0	17.0—18.0	12.5—16.5	9.5—12.0	< 9.5
16	> 19.0	17.5—19.0	13.5—17.0	10.0—13.0	< 10.0
17	> 19.5	18.0—19.5	13.5—17.5	10.5—13.0	< 10.0
18 – 24	> 23.5	19.25—23.50	16.75—19	13.25—16.5	0—13
25 – 36	> 18.75	15.50—18.75	13.25—15.25	8.50—13	0—8.25
36 – 49	> 17.25	13.50—17.25	11.25—13.25	7.75—11	0—7.5
Over 50	> 15.5	12—15.50	9.5—11.75	7.50—9.25	0—7.25
Female:					
6	> 16.5	16.0—16.5	13.0—15.5	11.5—12.5	< 11.5
7	> 17.0	16.5—17.0	13.5—16.0	11.5—13.0	< 11.5
8	> 17.0	16.5—17.0	13.0—16.0	11.0—12.5	< 11.0
9	> 17.0	16.5—17.0	13.0—16.0	11.0—12.5	< 11.0
10	> 17.5	17.0—17.5	13.5—16.5	10.5—13.0	< 10.5
11	> 18.0	17.0—18.0	13.5—16.5	11.5—13.0	< 11.5
12	> 19.0	17.5—19.0	14.5—17.0	12.0—14.0	< 12.0
13	> 20.0	18.5—20.0	14.5—18.0	12.0—14.0	< 12.0
14	> 19.5	19.0—19.5	15.5—18.5	12.5—15.0	< 12.5
15	> 20.0	19.5—20.0	16.0—19.0	13.5—15.5	< 13.5
16	> 20.5	19.5—20.5	16.5—19.0	14.0—16.0	< 14.0
17	> 20.5	19.5—20.5	16.0—19.0	13.5—15.5	< 13.5
18 – 24	> 21.5	19.75—21.5	17—19.5	13.75—16.75	0—13.5
25—36	> 18.25	16—18.25	14.25—15.75	9—14	0—8.75
36-49	> 18.5	15—18.5	12.25—14.75	9—12	0—8.75
Over 50	> 15.25	12.75—15.25	9.5—12.5	5.5—9.25	0—5.25

* Data from Ross et al (1985, 1987), Heyward (1998)

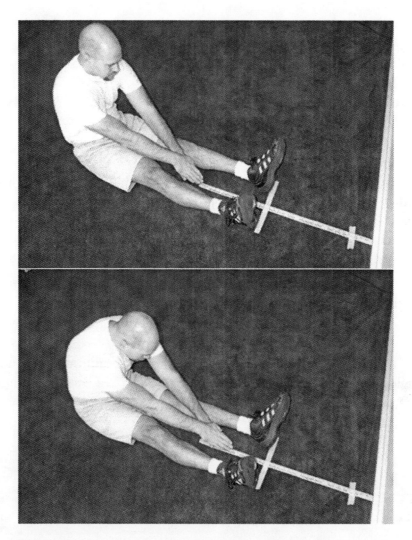

Figure 6.1—Modified Sit and Reach Test. TOP: Start – Hands on top of each other, feet at 15-inch mark. BOTTOM: Finish – reach as far out as possible, keeping knees straight.

GONIOMETER TESTS

For additional information see references 5, 21, 23

Equipment: Goniometer
Objective: To measure the passive flexibility of major joints.
Procedure:

There are several goniometers available commercially, or you may construct one using two straightedges and a circular piece of cardboard marked off in 1-degree increments (Figure 6.2).

1) Place the axis of the goniometer over the axis of the joint to be measured. The moveable arm of the goniometer is placed over the more movable body segment, while the fixed arm of the goniometer is placed in line with the more stationary body segment.

2) Record the reading on the goniometer with the joint in a relaxed position.

3) Have the examinee move the body segment through the full range of motion, and measure the joint angle at the end of the range of motion. Because this is a test of passive flexibility, meaning that the examinee must move the body segments voluntarily, do not force the body segment to further range of motion.

4) Record the measurements for each joint's beginning and ending angles. Examples of how to measure each joint are shown in Figures 6.3-6.8.

Figure 6.2—Standard Goniometer.

Scoring: Use Datasheet #22

Record the beginning and ending joint angles on Datasheet #22. Subtract the beginning joint angle from the ending joint angle, and record total range of motion (ROM) for each joint. Compare to Table 6.2.

Table 6.2

Average range of motion (ROM) of major joints for healthy adults.

Joint	Motion	ROM (degrees)	Motion	ROM (degrees)
Shoulder	Flexion	150-180	Extension	50-60
	Abduction	180	Adduction	40-50
Elbow	Flexion	140-150		
Wrist	Flexion	60-80	Extension	60-70
	Radial deviation	20	Ulnar deviation 30	
Hip	Flexion	100-120	Extension	30
	Abduction	40-45	Adduction	20-30
Knee	Flexion	135-150		
Ankle	Dorsiflexion	20	Plantar flexion	40-50

* Data from Green & Heckman (1994), ACSM (1998)

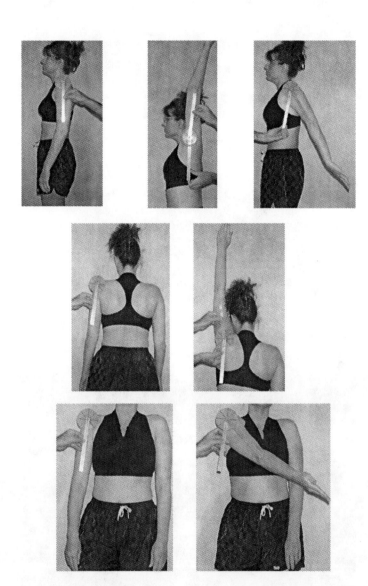

Figure 6.3—Shoulder Goniometer Measurements. TOP LEFT: Beginning Position for Flexion and Extension. TOP CENTER: Flexion measurement. TOP RIGHT: Extension measurement. MIDDLE LEFT: Beginning Abduction measurement. MIDDLE RIGHT: Abduction measurement. BOTTOM LEFT: Beginning Adduction measurement. BOT-TOM RIGHT: Adduction measurement.

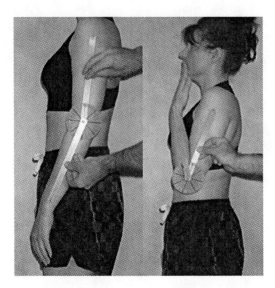

Figure 6.4—Elbow Goniometer Measurements. LEFT: Beginning Flexion measurement. RIGHT: Flexion measurement.

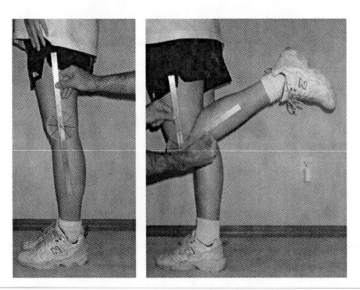

Figure 6.5—Knee Goniometer Measurements. LEFT: Beginning flexion measurement. RIGHT: Flexion measurement.

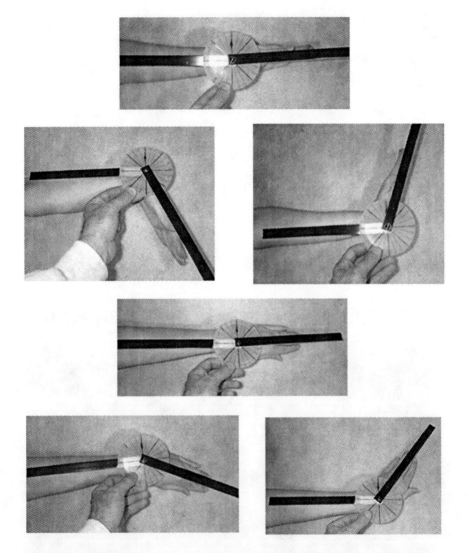

Figure 6.6—Wrist Goniometer Measurements. TOP: Beginning Flexion/Extension measurement. MIDDLE LEFT: Flexion measurement. MIDDLE RIGHT: Extension measurement. MIDDLE CENTER: Beginning Deviation measurement. BOTTOM LEFT: Radial deviation measurement. BOTTOM RIGHT: Ulnar deviation measurement.

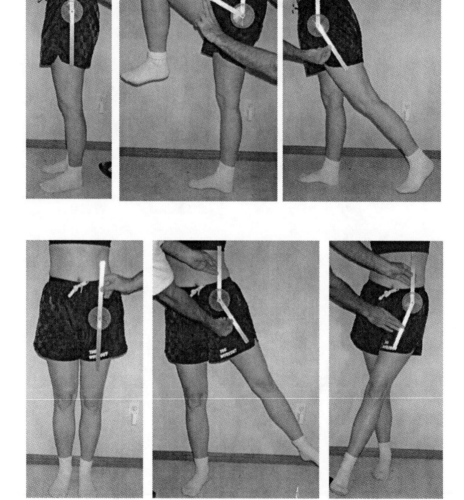

Figure 6.7—Hip Goniometer Measurements. TOP LEFT: Beginning measurement for flexion and extension. TOP CENTER: Flexion measurement. TOP RIGHT: Extension measurement. BOTTOM LEFT: Beginning measurement for adduction and abduction. BOTTOM CENTER: Abduction measurement. BOTTOM RIGHT: Adduction measurement.

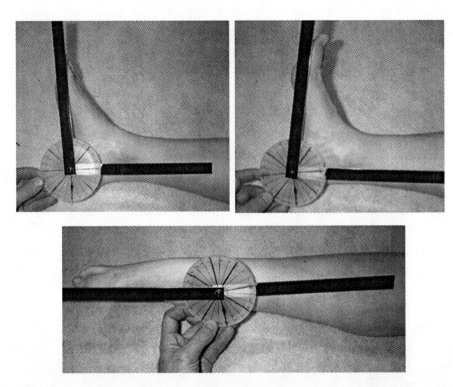

Figure 6.8—Ankle Goniometer Measurements. TOP LEFT: Beginning Measurement. TOP RIGHT: Dorsiflexion measurement. BOTTOM: Plantarflexion measurement.

Chapter 7:

Agility Tests

Agility is the ability to quickly accelerate, brake, change direction, and accelerate again. Tests of agility involve the examinee being able to move quickly to a predetermined position, change directions and move again. Before subjecting an examinee to agility tests, determine if they are able to make the sudden changes in direction and motion without unnecessary risk. For instance, agility tests would not be appropriate for an individual that has difficulty walking without the assistance of a cane or walker. Also, individuals with unstable ankles or feet may further injure these areas with the increased stress during agility testing. Finally, make sure that examinees are equipped with proper footwear before beginning agility training or testing.

Agility tests can be modified to increase difficulty by adding different elements into the course. For instance, a cone or mark on the floor can be placed at each intersection or direction change position. The examinee could be instructed to squat down and touch this point before changing direction and heading to the next point. Likewise, objects such as medicine balls can be carried and dropped or picked up at different points in the course. The possibilities are endless, and can be designed to add some sport specific elements to the tests. The scores provided are for use without any modifications to the directions.

MODIFIED EDGREN SIDE STEP TEST

For additional information see references 18, 25, 26, 30

Equipment: Masking tape, Stopwatch

Objective: To test the ability to move laterally and change directions quickly.

Procedure:

Place three lines approximately 6 feet long, parallel to each other and 8 feet apart (Figure 7.1).

1) The examinee stands straddling the centerline.

2) On the command "Ready, Go", start the stopwatch. The examinee sidesteps to the right until the right foot crosses the outside right line. The examinee then reverses direction and sidesteps to the left until the left foot crosses the outside left line. The examinee continues moving back and forth across the lines as fast as possible for 30 seconds. The examinee must face the same direction the entire test, and cannot cross the feet during the side-step movement.

3) Record the number of outside lines crossed in the 30 seconds.

4) Allow 5 minutes of rest. Repeat for a total of 3 trials.

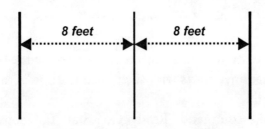

Figure 7.1- Line setup for Modified Edgren Side Step Test. Three lines parallel to each other, 8 feet apart.

Scoring: Use Datasheet #23

The score is the number of outside lines crossed in 30 seconds. Compare best score to Table 7.1.

Table 7.2					
	Excellent	**Good**	**Average**	**Fair**	**Low**
Men	<10.72	10.72-11.49	11.50-13.02	13.03-13.79	>13.79
Women	<12.19	12.19-12.99	13.00-13.90	13.91-14.49	>14.49

Scores for Semo Agility Test

* Data from Johnson & Nelson (1986)

SEMO AGILITY TEST

For additional information see references 27, 29

Equipment: Four plastic cones or other marking device, Stopwatch

Objective: To measure the ability to move sideways, backward and forward, and to change directions quickly.

Procedure:

The cones are placed to form a rectangle 12 feet by 19 feet, with the cones serving as the corners (Figure 7.2). If a basketball court is available, the cones can be placed inside the corners of the free-throw area.

1) The examinee starts with their back to cone "A" at the designated Start/Finish line.

2) Give the command "Ready, Go". Start the stopwatch when the examinee first moves. The examinee side steps from A to B, passes outside the cone; then backpedals from B to D, passes inside the cone; then sprints forward from D to A, passes outside the cone; then backpedals from A to C, passes inside the cone; then sprints forward from C to B, passes outside the cone; and finally side steps from B to the finish line. The directional arrows on Figure 7.2 show the correct pattern.

3) Stop the stopwatch when the examinee passes over the finish line.

4) Allow 5 minutes rest. Repeat test 2-3 times, recording elapsed time on datasheet #24.

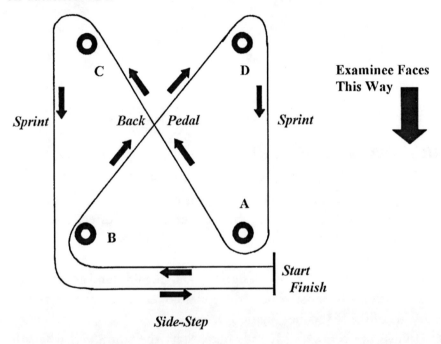

Figure 7.2—Course layout and movement directions for Semo Agility Test. Four cones are set-up so that the course is 12 feet wide (A to B) and 19 feet long (A to D). Masking tape can be used on the floor to indicate movement directions.

Scoring: Use Datasheet #24

The score is the best-recorded time to the nearest tenth of a second. Compare to Table 7.2.

Table 7.2. Scores for Semo Agility Test					
	Excellent	**Good**	**Average**	**Fair**	**Low**
Men	<10.72	10.72-11.49	11.50-13.02	13.03-13.79	>13.79
Women	<12.19	12.19-12.99	13.00-13.90	13.91-14.49	>14.49

* Data from Johnson & Nelson (1986)

RIGHT BOOMERANG RUN TEST

For additional information see references 19, 27, 33

Equipment: Four plastic cones or other marking device, Stopwatch.

Objective: To move through the course, changing directions several times, as fast as possible.

Procedure:

Place a cone 17 feet from a designated starting line, and another cone 15 feet beyond the first cone. Additional cones are placed 15 feet on each side of the first cone (Figure 7.3).

1) Give the command "Ready, Go". Start the stopwatch when the examinee begins moving. The examinee runs to the center cone, makes a quarter right turn; runs to cone A, makes a complete turn around it; runs to the center cone, makes a quarter right turn; runs to cone B, makes a complete turn around it; runs to the center cone, makes a quarter right turn; runs to cone C, makes a complete turn around it; runs to the center cone, makes a quarter turn and runs to the finish line. The directional arrows on Figure 7.3 show the correct pattern.

2) Stop the stopwatch when the examinee passes over the finish line.

3) Allow 5 minutes rest. Repeat for 3 trials.

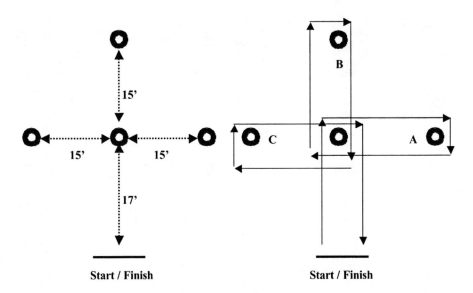

Figure 7.3—Right Boomerang Run Test. LEFT: Course layout. RIGHT: Movement directions.

Scoring: Use Datasheet #25

The score is the best-recorded time to the nearest tenth of a second. Compare to Table 7.3.

Table 7.3

Scores for Right Boomerang Run Test (Seconds)

	Excellent	Good	Average	Fair	Low
Men	<10.79	10.80-11.49	11.50-12.60	12.61-13.90	>13.90
Women	<12.60	12.60-12.99	13.00-14.59	14.60-15.99	>15.99

*Data from Johnson & Nelson (1986)

Chapter 8:

Kinesthesis Tests

Kinesthetic sense is the awareness of muscular movement and position. Receptors in the muscles, tendons, joints, and other body parts help control and coordinate motor patterns by sensing what the body is doing and sending that information to the brain. The eyes and visual sense provide a large amount of feedback about what the body is doing. When visual input is removed, you have to rely on the built-in receptors within the body to inform you about where your limbs are in space.

Tests of kinesthesis teach you to control your body and the amount of muscular force you generate. These tests involve the application of power, and movement of the body without visual input. Allow examinees to practice the movements involved in these tests before blindfolding them. The idea is to learn a motor pattern, and then repeat it while visually impaired. While these tests are not directly applicable to any sport or activity, they do provide interesting information on how well an examinee can control the application of power and muscular involvement.

Because examinees will be blindfolded, spotting is especially necessary. If you feel that an examinee is unstable without visual input, these tests should not be performed. Additionally, make sure that the testing area is clear of any obstacles that the examinee can stumble or trip over.

DISTANCE PERCEPTION JUMP TEST

For additional information see references 44, 45

Equipment: Blindfold, Masking tape, Measuring tape.

Objective: To test the ability to jump a specified distance without the use of sight (to know where the body is in space).

Procedure:

Use the masking tape to mark two lines on the floor, parallel to each other, either 2 or 3 feet apart depending on the ability of the examinee.

1) The examinee should stand with their toes touching one line, and attempt to jump over the next line and land with their heels touching the line (Figure 8.1).

2) The examinee is allowed one practice trial without the blindfold.

3) After the practice trial, secure the blindfold over the examinee's eyes and ensure that they cannot see down to the floor.

4) Place the examinee at the starting position and instruct them to attempt the jump exactly as before; the goal is to land with the heels touching the other line.

5) Upon landing, measure the distance (to the nearest ¼ inch) from the examinee's heels to the goal line.

6) Allow 3 trials.

Figure 8.1—Distance Perception Jump Test. TOP: Starting position, toes on the line. BOTTOM: Finish position, heels on the line.

Scoring: Use Datasheet #26

The score is the distance from the heels to the goal line for each attempt. If the examinee lands beyond the goal line, the score will be a positive number (i.e. +2 ½ inches); if the examinee lands before the goal line, the score will be a negative number (i.e. −1 ¼ inches). Add up the scores for all three trials. Positive and negative scores may cancel each other out. The best score is to land exactly on the line, and have the total score equal zero. Norms for this test are not available. Test-retest can be done to show improvement over time.

BASKETBALL FOUL SHOT TEST

For additional information see reference 25

Equipment: Basketball, Blindfold, Basketball goal.

Objective: To test the ability to place the basketball in the goal from a set distance without the use of sight.

Procedure:

1) The examinee stands at the foul line (or a closer distance if unable to reach the goal) and takes three practice shots.

2) Blindfold the examinee and ensure that they cannot see the goal.

3) The examinee is given five shots at placing the basketball in the goal. Any type of shooting style is acceptable (i.e. overhead or underhand), but the examinee cannot step over the foul line or the shot is disqualified.

Scoring: Use Datasheet #27

Points are awarded in the following manner:

* 3 points if the ball goes through the rim
* 2 points if the ball hits the rim but fails to go through
* 1 point if the ball hits the backboard but misses the rim
* 0 points if the ball misses the rim and backboard completely

The score is the total number of points for all five shots. Norms for this test are not available. Test-retest can be done to show improvement over time.

Chapter 9:

Balance Tests

Balancing the body involves the coordination of most of the skeletal muscles at one time. While some muscles are contracting and providing support, others are stabilizing joints or adjusting to counteract any movements. Balance is a very important part of fitness that is often overlooked. As an infant trying to become a toddler, balance must be learned before walking is possible. As we age, balance is often taken for granted, and then recognized as an important element of fitness when we become older and our balance is compromised.

When testing for balance, the examinee should be wearing good shoes, have stable ankles, and should be spotted closely. Training for balance quickly improves the scores on these tests. Other tests for balance can be designed using balance beams, rocker boards, or stability balls.

BASS DYNAMIC BALANCE TEST

For additional information see references 10, 27

Equipment: Stick (1 inch wide, 12 inches long), Masking tape, Stopwatch.

Objective: To test the ability to balance on the ball of one foot while standing on a reduced surface area.

Procedure:

This test can be performed two ways, with the stick in a Lengthwise position or a Crosswise position (Figure 9.1).

1) Tape the ends of the stick to the floor to prevent it from moving or rolling over.

2) Have the examinee place the ball of their dominant foot on the stick.

3) Start the stopwatch when the other foot leaves the ground.

4) Stop the stopwatch at the moment the foot contacts the ground, or the examinee steps off of the stick.

5) Repeat steps 3 and 4 using the non-dominant foot.

6) Allow 6 trials on each foot, recording the time in seconds.

Scoring: Use Datasheet #28

The score is the total amount of time in seconds the examinee was balanced on one foot. The final score is the total time of 6 trials on each foot. Compare to Table 9.1 for Crosswise test, Table 9.2 for Lengthwise test.

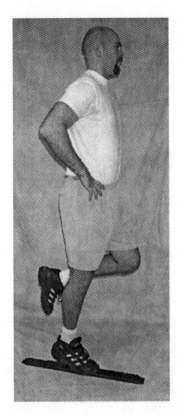 

Figure 9.1—Bass Dynamic Balance Test. LEFT: Stick in Lengthwise position. RIGHT: Stick in Crosswise position.

Table 9.1

Scores for Bass Dynamic Balance Test —Crosswise position (seconds)

	Excellent	Good	Average	Fair	Low
Men	> 224	165-224	65-164	15-64	0-14
Women	> 179	140-179	60-139	15-59	0-14

*Data from Johnson & Nelson (1986)

Table 9.2

Scores for Bass Dynamic Balance Test—Lengthwise position (seconds)

	Excellent	Good	Average	Fair	Low
Men	> 345	306-245	221-305	181-220	0-180
Women	> 335	301-335	206-300	166-205	0-165

*Data from Johnson & Nelson (1986)

STORK STAND TEST

For additional information see references 25, 27

Equipment: Stopwatch.

Objective: To test the ability to balance on one foot.

Procedure:

1) The examinee assumes a standing position on the dominant leg. The hands are placed on the hips, and the foot of the non-dominant leg is positioned on the inside of the knee of the dominant leg (Figure 9.2).

2) The test begins when the examinee raises the heel off of the ground and is balanced on the ball of the foot. Start the stopwatch when the heel leaves the ground.

3) Stop the stopwatch at the moment the heel contacts the ground.

4) Repeat using the non-dominant leg.

5) Allow 3 trials on each leg, alternating between dominant and non-dominant.

Scoring: Use Datasheet #29

The score for each trial is the time in seconds that balance was maintained. Final score is the best time of the three trials. Compare to Table 9.3.

Table 9.3					
Scores for Stork Stand Test (seconds)					
	Excellent	**Good**	**Average**	**Fair**	**Low**
Men	> 50	37-50	15-36	5-14	0-4
Women	> 27	23-27	8-22	3-7	0-2
*Data from Johnson & Nelson (1986)					

Figure 9.2—Stork Stand Test

Chapter 10:

Reaction Tests

Reaction involves recognizing a stimulus to move, and accelerating the body in a specific direction in as short a time as possible. These tests involve the tester giving visual cues to the examinee in the form of hand motions. The tests can be modified to make the examinee respond to different stiumuli, such as throwing a baseball in a specific direction for the examinee to field, or the tester moving in the given direction while the examinee follows. The use of these tests can be modified to your specific sport needs, or just to increase the difficulty when used as a training method.

When performing these tests, be consistent with your cues and movements. Do not attempt to trick or fool the examinee by adding "faking" moves.

NELSON CHOICE RESPONSE MOVEMENT TEST

For additional information see references 27, 35

Equipment: Stopwatch, Masking tape

Objective: To test the ability to make a decision based on a stimulus and move quickly in a given direction.

Procedure:

Mark three parallel lines 21 feet apart.

1) The examinee stands straddling the centerline, facing the examiner (Figure 10.1).

2) Hold the stopwatch overhead, give the command "Ready", pause for 1-2 seconds and then quickly wave your arm left or right, simultaneously starting the watch.

3) The examinee should run as quickly as possible in the direction the watch was moved.

4) Stop the watch when the examinee crosses the correct line. The time is recorded to the nearest tenth of a second. Should the examinee move in the wrong direction, they must reverse directions and run across the correct finish line.

5) A total of 10 trials, 5 to the left and 5 to the right, are given in random order. To ensure random order, write "Left" on 5 note cards, and "Right" on 5 note cards, and randomly draw them out of a box for each trial. A short rest between trials is allowed.

Scoring: Use Datasheet #30

The score is the time it takes for the examinee to move across the correct finish line, measured to the tenth of a second. Average the 10 trials and compare to Table 10.1.

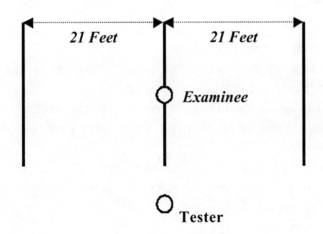

Figure 10.1—Floor area layout for Nelson Choice Response Movement Test

Table 10.1

Scores for Nelson Choice Response Movement Test (seconds)

	Excellent	Good	Average	Fair	Low
Men	< 1.3	1.3 – 1.6	1.7 – 2.4	2.5 – 2.7	> 2.7
Women	< 1.6	1.6 – 1.9	2.0 – 2.5	2.6 – 2.8	> 2.8

*Data from Johnson & Nelson (1986)

FOUR-WAY ALTERNATE RESPONSE TEST

For additional information see reference 25

Equipment: Stopwatch, Masking tape

Objective: To test the ability to make a decision based on a stimulus and move quickly in a given direction.

Procedure:

Mark four lines, each 15 feet from a central spot (Figure 10.2).

1) The examinee stands on the center spot, facing the examiner, who is outside the lines.

2) Hold the stopwatch directly in front of you, arm outstretched (pointing toward the examinee), give the command "Ready," pause for 1-2 seconds and then quickly wave your arm left, right, up or down; simultaneously starting the watch.

3) The examinee then runs as quickly as possible in the direction the watch was moved. If the tester waves his arm left or right, the examinee moves in that direction; if the tester moves his arm down, the examinee runs forward; if the tester moves his arm up, the examinee runs to the line behind them.

4) Stop the watch when the examinee crosses the correct line. The time is recorded to the nearest tenth of a second. Should the examinee move in the wrong direction, they must reverse directions and run across the correct finish line.

5) A total of 20 trials, 5 in each direction, are given in random order. To ensure random order, write "Left" on 5 note cards, "Right" on 5 note cards, "Forward" on 5 note cards, and "Back" on 5 note cards; and randomly draw them out of a box for each trial. A short rest between trials is allowed.

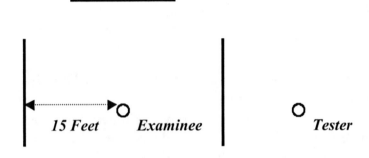

Figure 10.2—Floor area layout for Four-Way Alternate Response Test.

Scoring: Use Datasheet #31

The score is the time it takes for the examinee to move across the correct finish line, measured to the tenth of a second. Average the 20 trials. No norms are available for this test. Test-retest may be used to measure improvement.

Chapter 11:

Body Composition Estimates

Body composition is important to a person's overall health and to their ability to perform in their sport or activity. There are numerous ways of estimating body composition or bodyfat. Numerous different equations for estimating body fat with skinfold calipers have been developed. Additionally, techniques such as bioelectrical impedence, near infrared spectroscopy, hydrostatic weighing, body mass indexes, and other means of determining body composition are available. While each method has its positives and negatives, for the field tester, skinfold calipers are the most reliable and repeatable measure available.

The Jackson-Pollock 7-site skinfold equation is listed here, and while it is one of many equations that can be used, it has the most data for comparison, and is recognized as one of the most reliable equations for predicting body fat.

For those clients and athletes interested in outward appearance changes, and loss of inches, anthropometric measurements are available. While there are no norms available for circumference measurements, when used in conjunction with bodyfat estimates, they provide important information about how the body is proportioned, and changes that take place with a training program.

The largest source of error in bodyfat and circumference measurements is tester error. When taking measurements, it is best to mark the point being measured with a washable marker so that the same area is measured each time. Take several measurements and average to increase your accuracy. Taking photos during measurement may also assist you in measuring the same area during retests.

SKINFOLD BODY-FAT ESTIMATE

For additional information see references 6, 22, 24
Equipment: Skinfold calipers
Objective: To calculate estimated percent body-fat.
Procedure:
This skinfold technique uses the sum of seven sites for the calculation of estimated body-fat. All measurements should be made on the right side of the body.

1) Make a pinch by placing your thumb and forefinger approximately 2 inches apart, then squeeze and pull the skin together and slightly away from the body.

2) The calipers should be placed approximately 1 cm away from the thumb and finger making the pinch, perpendicular to the skinfold, and halfway between the crest and base of the fold.

3) Maintain the pinch while reading the caliper. Do not wait longer than 1-2 seconds before reading caliper, as holding the skinfold longer will compress the tissues.

4) To ensure accurate measurement, rotate through the measurement sites, retaking each site at least twice or until duplicate measurements are within 1-2 mm of each other.

Skinfold Site Descriptions:
Triceps – Vertical fold on the posterior midline of the upper arm, halfway between the acromion and olecranon processes, with the arm relaxed to the side of the body. Interpretation: Back of the upper arm, halfway from shoulder to elbow. See Figure 11.1.

Subscapular – Diagonal fold (45 degree angle) 1-2 cm below the inferior angle of the scapula. Interpretation: Just below and inside the scapula. See Figure 11.2.

Mid-axillary – Vertical fold on the mid-axillary line at the level of the xiphoid process of the sternum. Interpretation: Under the armpit, level with the bottom of the sterum. See Figure 11.3.

Chest – Diagonal fold one-half the distance (men) between the anterior axillary line and the nipple, or one third of the distance (women) between the anterior axillary line and the nipple. Interpretation: Men-halfway between crease of armpit and nipple. Women – one-third of way between crease of armpit and nipple. See Figure 11.4.

Suprailiac – Diagonal fold in line with the natural angle of the iliac crest taken in the anterior axillary line immediately superior to the iliac crest. Interpretation: Just above the hipbone. See Figure 11.5.

Abdominal – Vertical fold 2 cm to the right side of the umbilicus. Interpretation – Just to the right of the belly button. See Figure 11.6.

Thigh – Vertical fold on the anterior midline of the thigh, midway between the proximal border of the patella and the inguinal crease (hip). Interpretation: Halfway between the top of the kneecap and the crease in the hip. See Figure 11.7.

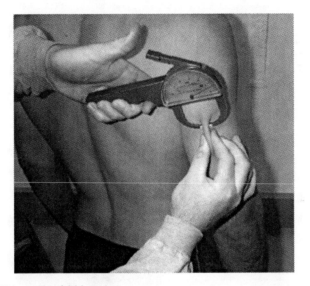

Figure 11.1—Triceps skinfold location.

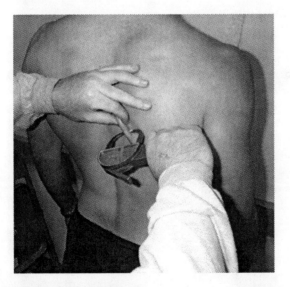

Figure 11.2—Subscapular skinfold location.

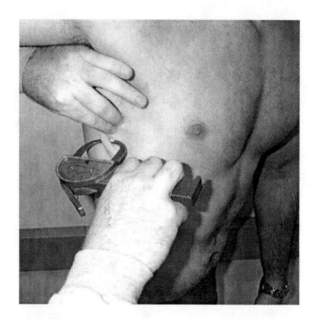

Figure 11.3—Mid-Axillary skinfold location.

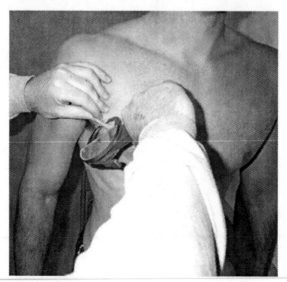

Figure 11.4—Chest skinfold location (male).

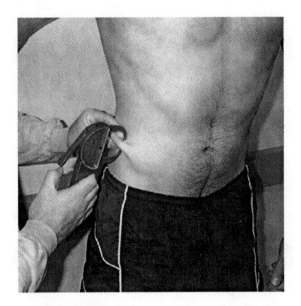

Figure 11.5—Suprailiac skinfold location.

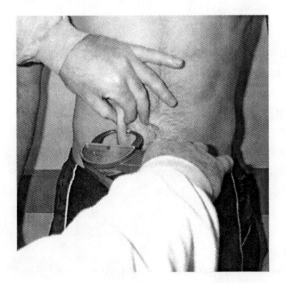

Figure 11.6—Abdominal skinfold location.

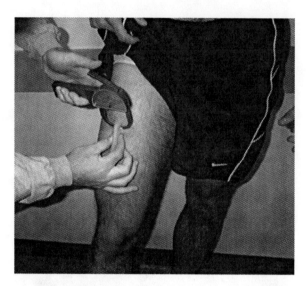

Figure 11.7—Thigh skinfold location.

Scoring: Use Datasheet #32

The score is obtained by summing the measurements from all seven sites, calculating body density, and then calculating percent body fat using the following equations. Compare to Table 11.1.

Body Density (Men) = 1.112 − 0.00043499 (Sum of 7 Skinfolds) + 0.00000055 (Sum of 7 Skinfolds)^2 − 0.00028826 (Age)
Body Density (Women) = 1.097 − 0.00046971 (Sum of 7 Skinfolds) + 0.00000056 (Sum of 7 Skinfolds)^2 − 0.00012828 (Age)
Percent Body Fat = (457 / Body Density) − 414.2

Example:
Male, 30 years old.
Skinfold Measurements: Triceps = 11, Subscapular = 14, Midaxillary = 9, Chest = 3, Suprailiac = 18, Abdominal = 20, Thigh = 17
Total skinfolds = 92

Body Density (Men) $= 1.112 - 0.00043499\ (92) + 0.00000055\ (92)^2$
$- 0.00028826\ (30)$
$= 1.112{-}0.040001908 + 0.00000000256036{-}$
0.0086478
$= 1.0634$ (rounded off to 4 decimal places)

Percent Body Fat $= (457\ /\ 1.0634) - 414.2$
$= 15.55$ (rounded off to 2 decimal places)

Estimated Body Fat $= 15.55\%$

Compare to Table 11.1 = Good

Table 11.1 Scores for Percent Body Fat					
Age:	**Excellent**	**Good**	**Average**	**Fair**	**Low**
Male					
20-29	<8.2	8.2—12.9	13—18.4	18.5—24.1	>24.1
30-39	<12.6	12.6—16.7	16.8—21.4	21.5—25.7	>25.7
40-49	<14.9	14.9—18.8	18.9—23.3	23.4—27.5	>27.5
50-59	<16.6	16.6—20.5	20.6—24.9	25—28.9	>28.9
60+	<16.8	16.8—21.1	21.2—25.8	25.9—29.8	>29.8
Female					
20-29	<15.8	15.8—19.8	19.9—24.5	24.6—29.9	>29.9
30-39	<16.7	16.7—20.8	20.9—25.9	26—31.1	>31.1
40-49	<16.9	16.9—24.2	24.3—29.1	29.2—33.5	>33.5
50-59	<23.3	23.3—27.5	27.6—32.5	32.6—36.7	>36.7
60+	<23.1	23.1—28.4	28.5—33.4	33.5—37.9	>37.9

*Data from ACSM 2000

ANTHROPOMETRIC MEASUREMENTS (BODY CIR-CUMFERENCE)

For additional information see references 12, 30, 27

Equipment: Gulick tape measure or cloth tape measure

Objective: To measure circumferences of different body segments.

Procedure:

When taking circumference measurements, it is important not to stretch the tape or cause the skin and tissue to be compressed.

1) Take three measurements at each site, paying attention to measure each site at the same location (you may want to mark the area where you are measuring). The examinee should be standing during the measurements. Use the tape measure to determine the circumference of each of the following sites to the nearest tenth of a centimeter.

Circumference Measurement Sites: (Figure 11.8)

Biceps – Measure the largest portion of the upper arm between the elbow and shoulder when the arm is maximally flexed and contracted.

Chest – Men: measure the distance around the chest at the level of the nipple.

Women: 1) measure the distance around the chest with the tape under the armpit and across the top of the breasts; or 2) measure the distance around the chest at the level of the nipple.

Abdomen – Measure the distance around the midsection at the level of the umbilicus (belly button).

Hip – Measure the distance around the body at the level of greatest protrusion of the buttocks.

Thigh —Measure the distance above the knee and below the groin, at the point of maximal circumference (usually at the top of the leg).

Scoring: Use Datasheet #33

Average the three measurements at each site. There are no norms for anthropometric measurements. Test and retest data can be used to show improvement over time.

Patrick S. Hagerman, Ed.D.

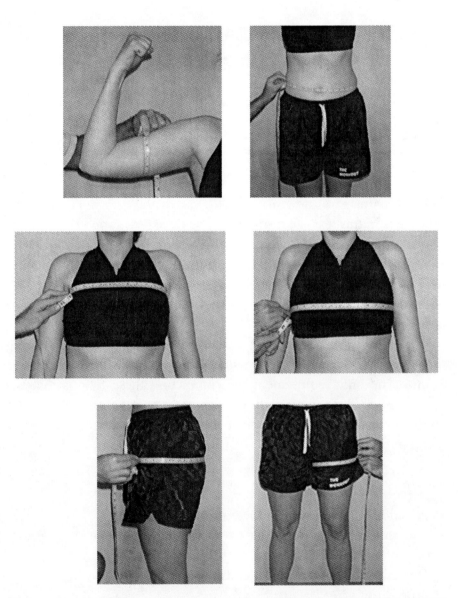

Figure 11.8—Circumference measurement sites. TOP LEFT: Biceps. TOP RIGHT: Abdomen. MIDDLE LEFT: Chest—Under armpits. MIDDLE RIGHT: Chest—Across the nipples. BOTTOM LEFT: Hips. BOTTOM RIGHT: Thigh.

Chapter 12:

Older Adult Fitness Battery

This test battery was designed for older adults 60-94 years of age. The other tests in this text can be used for this same population if the examinee is able to complete them; but the normative data supplied with most tests does not extend to this age group. The tests in this chapter have norms that extend from 60-94 years of age, and should not be used with younger populations. The tests can be performed individually, or as a complete battery.

These tests can be performed with minimal equipment, making them extremely suitable for on-site testing in retirement or nursing homes. The only requirement for completing these tests is that the examinee be able to move without the assistance of a cane or walker. Of course, pre-test screening is a must, and the supervision of a physician is recommended.

30-SECOND CHAIR STAND

For additional information see references 37, 38
Equipment: Stopwatch, Chair without arms (seat height approximately 17 inches).
Objective: Test the muscular endurance of the lower body.
Procedure:
1) Place the back of the chair against a wall for stability.

2) The examinee will begin in a seated position, arms folded across the chest. The examinee cannot use the arms and hands to help push to a standing position.

3) Give the command "Ready, Go". Start the stopwatch when the examinee begins moving. The examinee should rise to a full stand and return to the seated position as many times as possible in 30 seconds.

Scoring: Use Datasheet #34

The score is the number of competed repetitions (from seated to full stand) completed in 30 seconds. Compare to Table 12.1.

Table 12.1					
Scores for 30-Second Chair Stand **(number of repetitions completed)**					
	Excellent	**Good**	**Average**	**Fair**	**Low**
Male					
60-64	>21	19-21	16-18	14-15	<14
65-69	>20	18-20	15-17	12-14	<12
70-74	>19	17-19	15-16	12-14	<12
75-79	>18	17-18	14-16	11-13	<11
80-84	>17	15-17	12-14	10-11	<10
85-89	>16	14-16	11-13	8-10	<8
90-94	>14	12-14	10-11	7-9	<7
Female					
60-64	>19	17-19	15-16	12-14	<12
65-69	>17	16-17	14-15	11-13	<11
70-74	>17	15-17	13-14	10-12	<10
75-79	>17	15-17	12-14	10-11	<10
80-84	>15	14-15	11-13	9-10	<9
85-89	>14	13-14	10-12	8-9	<8
90-94	>13	11-13	8-10	4-7	<4

* Data from Rikli & Jones (1999)

6 MINUTE WALK TEST

For additional information see references 37, 38

Equipment: Stopwatch, 50 yard course
Objective: To assess aerobic endurance
Procedure:
This test is best performed on a marked, standard length track found at most public schools; or mark off the distance in a neighborhood using a long tape measure.

1) Give the command "Ready, Go". Have the examinee begin walking along the marked course for 6 minutes. Start the stopwatch when the examinee begins moving.

2) At the end of 6 minutes, note the total distance covered (yards) and record. Have the examinee sit and rest.

If at any time during the six minutes, the examinee may stop and rest before continuing. It may be a good idea to walk with the examinee if you feel that they may tire and need assistance.

Scoring: Use Datasheet #35
The score is the total distance covered in yards. Compare to Table 12.2.

	Excellent	Good	Average	Fair	Low
Table 12.2					
		Scores for 6-minute Walk			
		(number of yards completed)			
Male					
60-64	>789	735-789	610-734	555-609	<555
65-69	>764	700-764	560-699	500-559	<500
70-74	>744	680-744	545-679	480-544	<480
75-79	>714	640-714	470-639	395-469	<395
80-84	>679	605-679	445-604	370-444	<370
85-89	>659	570-659	380-569	295-379	<295
90-94	>589	500-589	305-499	215-304	<215
Female					
60-64	>709	660-709	545-659	495-544	<495
65-69	>694	635-694	500-634	440-499	<440
70-74	>674	615-674	480-614	420-479	<420
75-79	>654	585-654	430-584	365-429	<365
80-84	>609	540-609	385-539	310-384	<310
85-89	>594	510-594	340-509	260-339	<260
90-94	>519	440-519	275-439	195-274	<195

*Data from Rikli & Jones (1999)

2-MINUTE STEP-IN-PLACE TEST

For additional information see references 37, 38
Equipment: Stopwatch, Tape measure, Masking tape
Objective: To assess aerobic endurance
Procedure:

1) Determine the correct stepping height by measuring from the floor to the midway point between the examinee's patella (knee cap) and iliac crest (top of hip bone).

2) Use a piece of masking tape to mark the proper step height on an adjacent wall (Figure 12.1).

3) Instruct the examinee to "walk in place", lifting each knee to the height indicated on the wall, as many times as possible in 2 minutes.

3) Give the command "Ready, Go". Start the stopwatch when the examinee begins moving. Count the number of times the examinee lifts their knees to the determined height. If the knee does not reach the determined height, that repetition is disqualified.

Examinees may stop and rest during the 2-minutes, and resume stepping if time allows. Examinees can hold onto a wall or chair for balance if necessary.

4) At the end of the 2 minutes, have the examinee walk to cool down.

Scoring: Use Datasheet #36

The score is the total number of correct step repetitions completed in 2 minutes. Compare to Table 12.3.

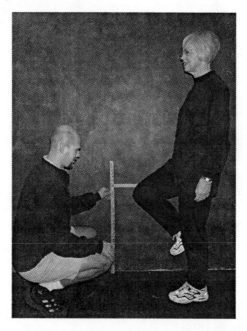

Figure 12.1—2 Minute Step-In-Place Test. Determine proper step height by measuring from the floor to the midpoint between the kneecap and the top of the hip-bone. Mark this location on the wall with tape.

ARM CURL TEST

For additional information see references 37, 38

Equipment: Stopwatch, Chair, 5 lb. dumbbell (women) or 8 lb. dumbbell (men)

Objective: To assess upper body strength

Procedure:

1) The examinee sits in the chair, back straight, feet flat on the floor, with the dominant side of the body close to the edge of the chair.

2) Have the examinee hold the dumbbell in the down position in the dominant arm. Instruct the examinee that on the "Go" command, to curl the dumbbell up as far as possible, and then return it to the down position. This counts as one repetition.

3) Give the command "Ready, Go", and start the stopwatch. Count the total number of correctly performed repetitions in 30-seconds.

The examiner may kneel beside the examinee and stabilize the upper arm by lightly holding the elbow to ensure that only the lower arm moves.

Scoring: Use Datasheet #37

The score is the number of completed repetitions in 30-seconds. Compare to Table 12.4

Table 12.3

Scores for 2-minute Step-in-Place Test
(number of repetitions completed)

	Excellent	Good	Average	Fair	Low
Male					
60-64	>127	115-127	87-114	74-86	<74
65-69	>129	116-129	86-115	72-85	<72
70-74	>124	110-124	80-109	66-79	<66
75-79	>124	109-124	73-108	56-72	<56
80-84	>117	103-117	71-102	56-70	<56
85-89	>105	91-105	59-90	44-58	<44
90-94	>101	86-101	52-85	36-51	<36
Female					
60-64	>121	107-121	75-106	60-74	<60
65-69	>122	107-122	73-106	57-72	<57
70-74	>115	101-115	68-100	53-67	<53
75-79	>114	100-114	68-99	52-67	<52
80-84	>103	91-103	60-90	46-59	<46
85-89	>97	85-97	55-84	42-54	<42
90-94	>84	72-84	44-71	31-43	<31

*Data from Rikli & Jones (1999)

Table 12.4

Scores for Arm Curl Test
(number of repetitions completed)

	Excellent	Good	Average	Fair	Low
Male					
60-64	>24	22-24	16-21	13-15	<13
65-69	>24	21-24	15-20	12-14	<12
70-74	>23	21-23	14-20	11-13	<11
75-79	>21	19-21	13-18	10-12	<10
80-84	>20	19-20	13-18	10-12	<10
85-89	>18	17-18	11-16	8-10	<8
90-94	>16	14-16	10-13	7-9	<7
Female					
60-64	>21	19-21	13-18	10-12	<10
65-69	>20	18-20	12-17	10-11	<10
70-74	>19	17-19	12-16	9-11	<9
75-79	>19	17-19	11-16	8-10	<8
80-84	>17	16-17	10-15	8-9	<8
85-89	>16	15-16	10-14	7-9	<7
90-94	>15	13-15	8-12	6-7	<6

*Data from Rikli & Jones (1999)

EIGHT FEET UP-AND-GO TEST

For additional information see references 37, 38

Equipment: Stopwatch, Chair, Cone or similar marker

Objective: To assess power, speed, agility, and dynamic balance

Procedure:

Position the chair back against a wall to stabilize it. Place a cone 8 feet away and directly in front of the chair. Remove any obstacles between the chair and the cone, and at least 4 feet beyond the cone.

1) The examinee sits in the chair, with their back against the back of the chair, hands on the thighs, feet flat on the floor.

2) Give the command "Ready, Go". Start the stopwatch when the examinee begins moving. The examinee should get up from the chair,

walk (don't run) as quickly as possible to the cone, turn and return to the chair and sit down. Stop the stopwatch when the examinee is seated.

3) Repeat for a total of 3 trials. Record the elapsed time to the nearest tenth of a second.

The examinee is allowed to use the hands to push off and out of the chair. The examiner should stand halfway between the chair and the cone to serve as a spotter.

Scoring: Use Datasheet #38

The score is the time it takes for the examinee to get up, circle the cone, and return to the seated position. Average the 3 trials. Compare to Table 12.5.

Table 12.5

Scores for Eight Feet Up-and-Go Test
(time to nearest tenth second)

	Excellent	Good	Average	Fair	Low
Male					
60-64	< 3.0	3.0—3.8	3.9—5.6	5.7—6.4	> 6.4
65-69	< 3.8	3.8—4.3	4.4—5.7	5.8—6.5	> 6.5
70-74	< 3.6	3.6—4.2	4.3—6.0	6.1—6.8	> 6.8
75-79	< 3.5	3.5—4.6	4.7—7.2	7.3—8.3	> 8.3
80-84	< 4.1	4.1—5.2	5.3—7.6	7.7—8.7	> 8.7
85-89	< 3.9	3.9—5.3	5.4—8.9	9.0—10.5	> 10.5
90-94	< 4.4	4.4—6.2	6.3—10.0	10.1—11.8	> 11.8
Female					
60-64	< 3.7	3.7—4.4	4.5—6.0	6.1—6.7	> 6.7
65-69	< 4.1	4.1—4.8	4.9—6.4	6.5—7.1	> 7.1
70-74	< 4.0	4.0—4.9	5.0—7.1	7.2—8.0	> 8.0
75-79	< 4.3	4.3—5.2	5.3—7.4	7.5—8.3	> 8.3
80-84	< 4.4	4.4—5.7	5.8—8.7	8.8—10.0	> 10.0
85-89	< 5.1	5.1—6.2	6.3—9.6	9.7—11.1	> 11.1
90-94	< 5.3	5.3—7.3	7.4—11.5	11.6—13.5	> 13.5

*Data from Rikli & Jones (1999)

CHAIR SIT AND REACH TEST

For additional information see references 37, 38
Equipment: Chair, Ruler
Objective: To test the flexibility of the lower back and hamstrings
Procedure:
Place the back of the chair against a wall for stability.

1) Have the examinee sit on the front edge of the chair so that the crease between the top of the leg and the buttocks is even with the edge of the seat. One leg should be extended straight in front of the hip with the heel on the floor and the toe in the air. The other leg should be bent with the foot flat on the floor (Figure 12.2).

2) Keeping the leg straight, have the examinee slowly bend forward and attempt to touch the toes of the extended leg by sliding the hands down the extended leg. The hands must be on top of each other, middle fingers touching.

3) Use the ruler to measure the distance the examinee is from touching the toes (negative number), or how far past their toes they were able to reach (positive number). Reaching the toes exactly results in a score of zero.

4) Repeat 3 times with each leg.

Scoring: Use Datasheet #39
The score is the average of the 3 trials. There will be a score for the left and right legs. Compare to Table 12.6.

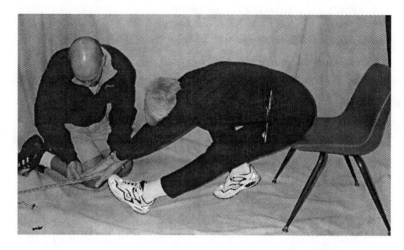

Figure 12.2—Chair Sit and Reach Test. Use a ruler to measure the distance from the fingers to the toes.

Table 12.6

Scores for Chair Sit and Reach Test
(inches)

	Excellent	Good	Average	Fair	Low
Male					
60-64	> 6.5	6.5—4.0	3.9—(-2.5)	(-2.6)—(-6.0)	> (-6.0)
65-69	> 6.0	6.0—3.0	2.9—(-3.0)	(-3.1)—(-6.0)	> (-6.0)
70-74	> 5.5	5.5—2.5	2.4—(-3.5)	(-3.6)—(-6.5)	> (-6.5)
75-79	> 5.0	5.0—2.0	1.9—(-4.0)	(-4.1)—(-7.0)	> (-7.0)
80-84	> 4.5	4.5—1.5	1.4—(-5.5)	(-5.6)—(-8.0)	> (-8.0)
85-89	> 3.0	3.0—0.5	0.4—(-5.5)	(-5.6)—(-8.0)	> (-8.0)
90-94	> 2.0	2.0—0.5	0.4—(-6.5)	(-6.6)—(-9.0)	> (-9.0)
Female					
60-64	> 7.0	7.0—5.0	4.9—(-0.5)	(-0.6)—(-3.0)	> (-3.0)
65-69	> 6.5	6.5—4.5	4.4—(-0.5)	(-0.6)—(-3.0)	> (-3.0)
70-74	> 6.0	6.0—4.0	3.9—(-1.0)	(-1.1)—(-3.5)	> (-3.5)
75-79	> 5.5	5.5—3.5	3.4—(-1.5)	(-1.6)—(-4.0)	> (-4.0)
80-84	> 5.0	5.0—3.0	2.9—(-2.0)	(-2.1)—(-4.5)	> (-4.5)
85-89	> 4.5	4.5—2.5	2.4—(-2.5)	(-2.6)—(-4.5)	> (-4.5)
90-94	> 3.5	3.5—1.0	0.9—(-4.5)	(-4.6)—(-7.0)	> (-7.0)

*Data from Rikli & Jones (1999)

BACK SCRATCH TEST

For additional information see references 37, 38
Equipment: Ruler
Objective: To test upper body flexibility
Procedure:

1) Have the examinee stand and reach over the shoulder of their dominant arm with their dominant hand (as if to scratch an itch); while reaching up behind the back with the other arm and hand in an attempt to touch or overlap the extended middle fingers of both hands (Figure 12.3).

2) Use the ruler to measure the distance between the middle fingers if they do not touch (negative score), or the amount of overlap of the middle fingers (positive score). Measure to the nearest half-inch.

3) Allow three trials.

Scoring: Use Datasheet #40
Average the three trials. Compare to Table 12.7.

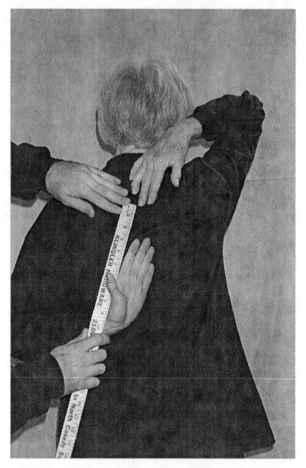

Figure 12.3—Back Scratch Test—Reach over the shoulder of the dominant hand, while reaching up behind the back with the other hand.

Table 12.7

Scores for Back Scratch Test
(inches)

	Excellent	Good	Average	Fair	Low
Male					
60-64	> 2.5	2.5—0.0	(-0.5)—(-6.5)	(-7.0)—(-10.0)	> (-10.0)
65-69	> 2.0	2.0—(-1.0)	(-1.5)—(-7.5)	(-8.0)—(-10.5)	> (-10.5)
70-74	> 2.0	2.0—(-1.0)	(-1.5)—(-8.0)	(-8.5)—(-11.0)	> (-11.0)
75-79	> 1.0	1.0—(-2.0)	(-2.5)—(-9.0)	(-9.5)—(-12.0)	> (-12.0)
80-84	> 1.0	1.0—(-2.0)	(-2.5)—(-9.5)	(-10.0)—(-12.5)	> (-12.5)
85-89	> 0.0	0.0—(-3.0)	(-3.5)—(-10.0)	(-10.5)—(-12.5)	> (-12.5)
90-94	> (-1.0)	(-1.0)—(-4.0)	(-4.5)—(-10.5)	(-11.0)—(-13.5)	> (-13.5)
Female					
60-64	> 4.0	4.0—1.5	1.0—(-3.0)	(-3.5)—(-5.5)	> (-5.5)
65-69	> 3.5	3.5—1.5	1.0—(-3.5)	(-4.0)—(-6.0)	> (-6.0)
70-74	> 3.0	3.0—1.0	0.5—(-4.0)	(-4.5)—(-6.5)	> (-6.5)
75-79	> 3.0	3.0—0.5	0.0—(-5.0)	(-5.5)—(-7.5)	> (-7.5)
80-84	> 2.5	2.5—0.0	(-0.5)—(-5.5)	(-6.0)—(-8.0)	> (-8.0)
85-89	> 2.0	2.0—(-1.0)	(-1.5)—(-7.0)	(-7.5)—(-10.0)	> (-10.0)
90-94	> 2.0	2.0—(-1.0)	(-1.5)—(-8.0)	(-8.5)—(-11.5)	> (-11.5)

*Data from Rikli & Jones (1999)

Appendix A: Test DataSheets

DATASHEET #1: ASTRAND-RHYMING CYCLE TEST

Name:_____ Age:_____ Date:_____
Weight:_____lbs. _____kg (lb/2.2)
Final Exercise Workload:_____Watts

Exercise Heart Rates per Test Minute:
1._____ 2._____ 3._____ 4._____ 5._____
6._____ 7._____ 8._____ 9._____ 10._____

Scoring:
1) Average the last two heart rates (those that were within 5 beats per minute of each other).
   (HR1_____ + HR2_____) / 2 = _____
   Average Heart Rate
2) Compare this heart rate and the exercise workload to Table 2.3 or Table 2.4 to find VO2.
   VO2 (l/min) from Table = _____
3) Multiply VO2 (l/min) by 1000.
   VO2 (l/min)_____ x 1000 = _____VO2 (ml/min)
4) Divide by the examinee's weight in kg.
   VO2 (ml/min)_____ / kg_____ = VO2 (ml/kg/min)_____
5) Multiply by the age correction factor using the closest age in Table 2.1.
   VO2 (ml/kg/min)_____ x Age correction factor _____
   = _____
6) Compare estimated VO2 max to Table 2.2.

Rating = LOW   FAIR   AVERAGE   GOOD   EXCELLENT

DATASHEET #2: YMCA PHYSICAL WORKING

CAPACITY TEST

Name:_____ Age:_____ Date:_____

Weight:_____lbs _____ Kg

Workload #1 = 25 Watts   HR1_____   HR2_____

Average HR_____

Workload #2 = _____ Watts HR1_____   HR2_____

Average HR_____

Workload #3 = _____ Watts HR1_____   HR2_____

Average HR_____

Workload #4 = _____ Watts HR1_____   HR2_____

Average HR_____

Estimated Maximum HR (220-age) = _____

Estimated Maximum Workload = _____ Watts

      1) Multiply max Watts by 12: _____ Watts x 12 = _____.

      2) Multiply bodyweight in Kg by 3.5: Weight _____ Kg x 3.5
        = _____.

      3) Add results of 1 and 2 above: _____ + _____ =
        _____

      4) Divide result by bodyweight in Kg: _____ / _____ Kg =
        _____.

      5) Compare estimated VO2 max to Table 2.2.

Rating = LOW   FAIR   AVERAGE   GOOD   EXCELLENT

YMCA Physical Working Capacity Test – Maximal Workload Extrapolation

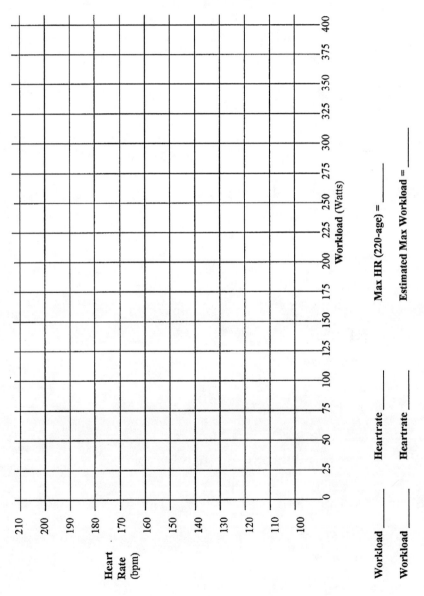

DATASHEET #3: COOPER 12-MINUTE RUN/WALK TEST

Name:_____ Age:_____ Date:_____

Distance covered in 12 minutes: _____ Miles

    1) Multiply distance covered (in decimal form) by 35.9712:

       _____ Miles x 35.9712 = _____

    2) Subtract 11.2872 from result:

       _____—11.2872 = _____

    3) Compare estimated VO2 max to Table 2.2.

Rating = LOW   FAIR   AVERAGE   GOOD   EXCELLENT

DATASHEET #4: 1.5 MILE RUN

Name:_____ Age:_____ Date:_____

Time to complete 1.5 miles:_____Minutes

    1) Divide 2413.5 by time to complete 1.5 miles:

       2413.5 / _____ Min. = _____

    2) Multiply result by 0.2:

       _____ x 0.2 = _____

    3) Add 3.5 to result:

       _____ + 3.5 = _____

    4) Compare estimated VO2 max to Table 2.2.

Rating = LOW   FAIR   AVERAGE   GOOD   EXCELLENT

DATASHEET #5: YOUTH DISTANCE RUN TEST

Name:_____ Age:_____ Date:_____
Time to complete distance: _____ Min _____ Sec
Compare to Table 2.6.
Rating = LOW   FAIR   AVERAGE   GOOD   EXCELLENT

DATASHEET #6: ROCKPORT WALK TEST

Name:_____ Age:_____ Date:_____
Weight:_____ lbs.   Male or Female
Time to Complete 1 mile:_____ Minutes   Final Heart
Rate:_____(bpm)
Calculate:

                                                    132.853

1) 0.0769 x weight in pounds   - _____
2) 0.3877 x age in years   - _____
3) 6.315 x gender (Male = 1, Female = 2) + _____
4) 3.2649 x time to complete 1 mile   - _____
5) 0.1565 x final heart rate   - _____
                                           =_____
6) Compare estimated VO2 max to Table 2.2.

   Rating = LOW   FAIR   AVERAGE   GOOD   EXCELLENT

DATASHEET #7: HARVARD STEP TEST

Name:_____ Age:_____ Date:_____

Time completed:_____ Minutes / Seconds

Number of heart beats from 1 to 1 ½ minutes after exercise: _____ beats

Score from Table 2.4: _____

Interpretation: LOW   AVERAGE   GOOD

DATASHEET #8: QUEENS COLLEGE STEP TEST

Name:_____ Age:_____ Date:_____

Post-exercise heart rate:_____ beats per minute

1) Calculation:

Males: 0.42 x beats per minute = _____

111.33 – (above result) _____ = _____

Females: 0.185 x beats per minute = _____

65.81 – (above result) _____ = _____

2) Compare estimated VO2 max to Table 2.2.

Rating = LOW   FAIR   AVERAGE   GOOD   EXCELLENT

DATASHEET #9: YMCA BENCH PRESS TEST

Name:_____ Date:_____

Number of repetitions completed:_____

Compare to Table 3.1.

Rating: LOW   FAIR   AVERAGE   GOOD   EXCELLENT

DATASHEET #10: ISOMETRIC LEG SQUAT (WALL SIT) TEST

Name:_____   Date:_____
Time:_____ Minutes/Seconds

DATASHEET #11: PULL-UP TEST

Name:_____   Date:_____
Number of repetitions:_____
Compare to Table 3.2.

    Rating: LOW   FAIR   AVERAGE   GOOD   EXCELLENT

DATASHEET #12: SIT-UPS TEST

Name:_____   Date:_____
Number of repetitions:_____
Youth: Compare to Table 3.3.

    Rating: LOW   FAIR   AVERAGE   GOOD   EXCELLENT

Adult: Compare to Table 3.4.

Rating:
LOW   FAIR   BELOW   AVERAGE   ABOVE   GOOD   EXCELLENT
             AVERAGE   AVERAGE

DATASHEET #13: PUSH-UP TEST

Name:_____   Date:_____
Number of Repetitions: _____
Compare to Table 3.5 (Youth) or Table 3.6 (Adult)
Rating: LOW   FAIR   AVERAGE   GOOD   EXCELLENT

DATASHEET #14: DYNAMIC MUSCULAR ENDURANCE TEST BATTERY

Name:_____   Date:_____

Body weight:_____ pounds

Exercise:	Weight used:	Repetitions (max = 15)
Arm Curl	_____	_____
Bench Press	_____	_____
Lat Pull-down	_____	_____
Triceps Extension	_____	_____
Leg Extension	_____	_____
Leg Curl	_____	_____
Bent-knee Sit-up	Body weight	_____

Total Repetitions =   _____   (max = 105)

Compare to Table 3.7.

Rating:

LOW   FAIR   AVERAGE   GOOD   VERY GOOD   EXCELLENT

DATASHEET #15: 1-REP MAX TESTS

Name:_____   Date:_____

Exercise:_____

Procedure #1:
Warm-Up Set #1: Weight = _____ (7-10 repetitions)
Warm-Up Set #2: Weight = _____ (3-6 repetitions)
Warm-Up Set #3: Weight = _____ (2-3 repetitions)
1-Rep Max: Attempt #1 Weight = _____
1-Rep Max: Attempt #2 Weight = _____
1-Rep Max: Attempt #3 Weight = _____
Final 1-Rep Max = _____

Procedure #2:
10 RM Weight = _____
Estimated 1RM = 10RM Weight / 0.67 = _____
1-Rep Max: Attempt #1 Weight = _____
1-Rep Max: Attempt #2 Weight = _____
1-Rep Max: Attempt #3 Weight = _____
Final 1-Rep Max = _____

DATASHEET #16: MEDICINE BALL PUT TEST

Name:_____   Date:_____

Distance: Trial #1 _____   Trial #2 _____   Trial #3 _____

Compare to Table 4.1.

Rating: LOW   FAIR   AVERAGE   GOOD   EXCELLENT

DATASHEET #17: STANDING LONG JUMP TEST

Name:_____   Date:_____

Distance: 1)_____   2)_____   3)_____

Compare to Table 4.2.

Rating: LOW   FAIR   AVERAGE   GOOD   EXCELLENT

DATASHEET #18: VERTICAL JUMP TEST

Name:_____   Date:_____

Distance (inches): #1_____   #2_____   #3_____

Compare to Table 4.3.

Rating: LOW   FAIR   AVERAGE   GOOD   EXCELLENT

DATASHEET #19: 4-SECOND or 6-SECOND DASH

Name:_____   Date:_____

Distance (feet): #1_____   #2_____   #3_____

Compare to Table 5.1 (4-second dash) or Table 5.2 (6-second dash).

Rating: LOW   FAIR   AVERAGE   GOOD   EXCELLENT

DATASHEET #20: 50-YARD DASH

Name:_____   Date:_____

Time (to tenth of a second): #1_____   #2_____   #3_____

Compare to Table 5.3.

Rating: LOW   FAIR   AVERAGE   GOOD   EXCELLENT

DATASHEET #21: MODIFIED SIT AND REACH TEST

Name:_____   Date:_____

Distance to nearest ¼ inch: 1:_____   2:_____   3:_____

Compare to Table 6.1.

Rating: LOW   FAIR   AVERAGE   GOOD   EXCELLENT

DATASHEET #22: GONIOMETER TESTS

Name:_____   Date:_____

Joint:	Starting Angle:	Ending Angle:	ROM:	Average	
Shoulder Flexion				Y	N
Shoulder Extension				Y	N
Shoulder Abduction				Y	N
Shoulder Adduction				Y	N
Elbow Flexion				Y	N
Wrist Flexion				Y	N
Wrist Extension				Y	N
Wrist Radial Deviation				Y	N
Wrist Ulnar Deviation				Y	N
Hip Flexion				Y	N
Hip Extension				Y	N
Hip Abduction				Y	N
Hip Adduction				Y	N
Knee Flexion				Y	N
Ankle Dorsiflexion				Y	N
Ankle Plantar Flexion				Y	N

DATASHEET #23: MODIFIED EDGREN SIDE STEP TEST

Name:_____ Date:_____

Number of outside lines crossed:

Trial 1:_____ Trial 2:_____ Trial 3:_____

Compare to Table 7.1.

Rating: LOW   FAIR   AVERAGE   GOOD   EXCELLENT

DATASHEET #24: SEMO AGILITY TEST

Name:_____ Date:_____

Elapsed Time: #1_____ #2_____#3_____

Compare to Table 7.2.

Rating: LOW   FAIR   AVERAGE   GOOD   EXCELLENT

DATASHEET #25: RIGHT BOOMERANG RUN TEST

Name:_____ Date:_____

Elapsed Time: #1_____ #2_____#3_____

Compare to Table 7.3

Rating: LOW   FAIR   AVERAGE   GOOD   EXCELLENT

DATASHEET #26: DISTANCE PERCEPTION JUMP TEST

Name:_____ Date:_____

Distance from goal line: #1_____ #2_____ #3_____

Total Distance:_____

DATASHEET #27: BASKETBALL FOUL SHOT TEST

Name:_____   Date:_____

Points: Shot #1_____   #2_____   #3_____   #4_____   #5_____

Total Points:_____

DATASHEET #28: BASS DYNAMIC BALANCE TEST

Name:_____   Date:_____

Time in Seconds:

Crosswise: #1_____   #2_____   #3_____   #4_____

       #5_____   #6_____

Total Time:_____   Compare to Table 9.1

Rating: LOW   FAIR   AVERAGE   GOOD   EXCELLENT

Lengthwise: #1_____   #2_____   #3_____   #4_____

       #5_____   #6_____

Total Time:_____   Compare to Table 9.2

Rating: LOW   FAIR   AVERAGE   GOOD   EXCELLENT

DATASHEET #29: STORK STAND TEST

Name:_____   Date:_____

Trial #1:_____ seconds   #2_____seconds   #3_____seconds

Compare to Table 9.3.

Rating: LOW   FAIR   AVERAGE   GOOD   EXCELLENT

DATASHEET #30: NELSON CHOICE RESPONSE MOVEMENT TEST

Name:_____ Date:_____

Direction, and Time to nearest tenth of a second.

Trial #1:_____ L R #2_____ L R #3_____ L R #4_____ L R
   #5_____ L R #6:_____ L R #7_____ L R #8_____ L R
   #9_____ L R #10_____ L R

Average time:_____

Compare to Table 10.1

Rating: LOW   FAIR   AVERAGE   GOOD   EXCELLENT

DATASHEET #31: FOUR-WAY ALTERNATE RESPONSE TEST

Name:_____ Date:_____

Direction and Time to nearest tenth:

Trial #1:_____ L R F B	Trial #2:_____ L R F B
Trial #3:_____ L R F B	Trial #4:_____ L R F B
Trial #5:_____ L R F B	Trial #6:_____ L R F B
Trial #7:_____ L R F B	Trial #8:_____ L R F B
Trial #9:_____ L R F B	Trial #10:_____ L R F B
Trial #11:_____ L R F B	Trial #12:_____ L R F B
Trial #13:_____ L R F B	Trial #14:_____ L R F B
Trial #15:_____ L R F B	Trial #16:_____ L R F B
Trial #17:_____ L R F B	Trial #18:_____ L R F B
Trial #19:_____ L R F B	Trial #20:_____ L R F B

Average of 20 Trials:_____

DATASHEET #32: SKINFOLD BODY FAT TEST

Name:_____   Date:_____

Age:_____

1) Skinfold Measurements (mm):

Triceps: _____   Subscapular: _____

Midaxillary: _____   Chest: _____

Suprailiac: _____   Abdominal: _____

Thigh: _____
Total of 7 sites:_____

2) Calculate Body Density:

Men: 1.112

- 0.00043499 x _____Total Skinfolds

+ 0.00000055 x _____Total Skinfolds^2

- 0.00028826 x _____Age

Women: 1.097

- 0.00046971 x _____Total Skinfolds

+ 0.00000056 x _____Total Skinfolds^2

- 0.00012828 x _____ Age

3) Calculate Percent Body Fat:

Percent Body Fat = (457 /_____ Body Density) − 414.2 =

_____

4) Compare to Table 11.1:

Rating: LOW   FAIR   AVERAGE   GOOD   EXCELLENT

DATASHEET #33: ANTHROPOMETRIC MEASURE-MENTS

Name:_____ Date:_____

Age:_____ Weight:_____ Height:_____

Biceps: #1_____ #2_____ #3_____ Average:_____

Chest: #1_____ #2_____ #3_____ Average:_____

Abdomen: #1_____ #2_____ #3_____ Average:_____

Hip: #1_____ #2_____ #3_____ Average:_____

Thigh: #1_____ #2_____ #3_____ Average:_____

DATASHEET #34: 30-SECOND CHAIR STAND

Name:_____ Date:_____

Number of complete repetitions in 30-seconds = _____

Compare to Table 12.1

Rating: LOW   FAIR   AVERAGE   GOOD   EXCELLENT

DATASHEET # 35: 6-MINUTE WALK

Name:_____ Date:_____

Total distance covered: _____ yards

Compare to Table 12.2

Rating: LOW   FAIR   AVERAGE   GOOD   EXCELLENT

DATASHEET #36: 2-MINUTE STEP-IN-PLACE

Name:_____ Date:_____

Stepping Height: _____ inches

Number of correct repetitions:_____

Compare to Table 12.3

Rating: LOW   FAIR   AVERAGE   GOOD   EXCELLENT

DATASHEET #37: ARM CURL

Name:_____   Date:_____
Number of correct repetitions:_____
Compare to Table 12.4

Rating: LOW   FAIR   AVERAGE   GOOD   EXCELLENT

DATASHEET #38: EIGHT FEET UP-AND-GO

Name:_____   Date:_____
Time #1: _____ seconds
Time #2: _____ seconds
Time #3: _____ seconds
Average time:_____ seconds
Compare to Table 12.5

Rating: LOW   FAIR   AVERAGE   GOOD   EXCELLENT

DATASHEET #39: CHAIR SIT AND REACH

Name:_____   Date:_____
Left Leg: Trial #1_____   Trial #2_____   Trial #3_____
Right Leg: Trial #1_____   Trial #2_____   Trial #3_____
Average Left Leg:_____
Average Right Leg:_____
Compare to Table 12.6

Rating Left Leg: LOW   FAIR   AVERAGE   GOOD   EXCELLENT
Rating Right Leg: LOW   FAIR   AVERAGE   GOOD   EXCELLENT

DATASHEET #40: BACK SCRATCH

Name:_____   Date:_____
Trial #1: _____   Trial #3: _____   Trial #4: _____
Average: _____
Compare to Table 12.7

Rating: LOW   FAIR   AVERAGE   GOOD   EXCELLENT

References

1. AAHPER-NEA, Fitness Dept (1976). *AAHPER Youth Fitness Test Manual.*

2. AAHPERD (1976). *Youth fitness test manual.* Reston, VA: AAHPERD

3. AAHPERD (1980). *AAHPERD Health related physical fitness test manual.* Reston, VA: American Alliance for Health, Physical Education, and Recreation.

4. American College of Sports Medicine (1995). *Guidelines for Exercise Testing and Prescription* (5th Ed.). Philadelphia: Williams and Wilkins

5. American College of Sports Medicine (1998). *ACSM's Resource Manual for Guidelines for Exercise Testing and Prescription* (3rd Ed.). Philadelphia: Lippincott, Williams and Wilkins

6. American College of Sports Medicine (2000). *ACSM's Guidelines for Exercise Testing and Prescription* (6th Ed.). Philadelphia: Lippincott Williams and Wilkins

7. Astrand, I. (1960). Aerobic work capacity in men and women with special reference to age. Acta. Physiol. Scand., 49(Suppl. 169)

8. Astrand, P.O., Rhyming, I. (1954). A nomogram for calculation of aerobic capacity (physical fitness) from pulse rate during submaximal work. Journal of Applied Physiology, 7:218-221.

9. Astrand, P.O., Rodahl, K. (1970). *Textbook of Work Physiology.* New York: McGraw-Hill, Inc.

10. Bass, R.I. (1939). An analysis of the components of tests of semicircular canal function and of static and dynamic balance. Research Quarterly, 10:33

11. Baumgartner, T.A., Jackson, A.S. (1987). *Measurement for evaluation in physical education and exercise science* (3rd Ed.). Dubuque: Wm.C. Brown

12. Baumgartner, T.A., Jackson, A.S. (1995). *Measurement for evaluation in physical education and exercise science* (5th Ed.). Dubuque: Wm.C. Brown

13. Brouha, L. (1943). The step test: A simple method of measuring physical fitness for muscular work in young men. Research Quarterly, 14(1):31-36

14. Chrysler Fund-AAU Physical Fitness Program (1990). *1989-1990 test manual.* Bloomington, IN: Amateur Athletic Union

15. Cooper, K.H. (1970). *The New Aerobics.* New York: M. Evans and Co., Inc.

16. Cooper, K.H. (1977). *The aerobics way.* New York: M. Evans and Co.

17. deVries, H.A. (1986). *Physiology of Exercise* (4th Ed.). Dubuque: Wm. C. Brown

18. Edgren, H.D. (1932). An experiment in the testing of ability and progress in basketball. Research Quarterly, 3(1): 159-171

19. Gates, D.D., Sheffield, R.P. (1940). Tests of change of direction as measurements of different kinds of motor ability in boys of the seventh, eighth, and ninth grades. Research Quarterly, 11:136-147.

20. Golding, L.A., Myers, C.R., and Sinning, W.E. (1989). *Y's way to physical fitness: The complete guide to fitness testing and instruction.* Champaign, IL: Human Kinetics

21. Greene, W.B., Heckman, J.D. (1994). *The clinical measurement of joint motion.* Rosemont, IL: American Academy of Orthopedic Surgeons

22. Heyward, V.H., Stolarczyk, L.M. (1996). *Applied body composition assessment.* Champaign, IL: Human Kinetics

23. Heyward, V.H. (1998). *Advanced fitness assessment and exercise prescription* (3rd Ed.). Champaign, IL: Human Kinetics

24. Jackson, A.S., Pollock, M.L. (1985). Practical assessment of body composition. Physician and Sportsmedicine. 13:76-90

25. Jensen, C.R., Hirst, C.C. (1980). *Measurement in physical education and athletics.* New York: Macmillan

26. Johnson, B.L., Nelson, J.K. (1979). *Practical measurements for evaluation in physical education.* Edina, MN: Burgess

27. Johnson, B.L., Nelson, J.K. (1986). *Practical measurements for evaluation in physical education* (4th ed). Edina, MN: Burgess

28. Katch, F.I., McArdle, W.D. (1983). *Nutrition, Weight Control, and Exercise* (2nd Ed.). Philadelphia: Lea & Febriger

29. Kirby, R.F. (1971). A simple measure of agility. Coach and Athlete, 32(11):30-31.

30. Kirkendall, D.R., Gruber, J.J., Johnson, R.E. (1987). *Measurement and evaluation for physical educators* (2nd Ed.). Champaign: Human Kinetics

31. Kline, G.M. et al (1987). Estimation of VO2 max from a one-mile track walk, gender, age, and body weight. Medicine and Science in Sports and Exercise, 19:253-259

32. Matthews, D.K. (1978). *Measurement in physical education* (5th Ed.). Philadelphia: W.B. Saunders

33. McCloy, C.H., Young, N.D. (1954). *Tests and measurements in physical education.* New York: Appleton Century-Crofts

34. Morrow, J.R. (2000). Measurement and evaluation in human performance. Champaign, IL: Human Kinetics

35. Nelson, J.K. (1967). Development of a practical performance test combining reaction time, speed of movement and choice of response. Unpublished study, Louisiana State University.

36. Nieman, D.C. (1990). *Fitness and Sports Medicine: An Introduction.* Palo Alto, CA: Bull

37. Rikli, R.E., Jones, C.J. (1999). Fitness Tests for community residing older adults, ages 60-94. Journal of Aging and Physical Activity, 7:129-161.

38. Rikli, R.E., Jones, C.J. (1999). Functional fitness normative scores for community residing older adults, ages 60-94. Journal of Aging and Physical Activity, 7:162-181

39. Rockport (1989). *The Rockport guide to fitness walking.* Marlboro, MA.

40. Ross, Dotson, Gilbert, Katz (1985). NCYFS I. Journal of Physical Education, Recreation and Dance. 56(1): 62-66

41. Ross, Dotson, Gilbert, Katz (1987). NCYFS II. Journal of Physical Education, Recreation and Dance. 58(9): 66-70

42. Safrit, M.J. (1986). *Introduction to measurement in physical education and exercise science.* St. Louis: Times Mirror

43. Safrit, M.J. (1990). *Introduction to measurement in physical education and exercise science.* St. Louis: Times Mirror/Mosby

44. Scott, M.G. (1955). Tests of kinesthesis. Research Quarterly, 26:234-241

45. Scott, M.G., French, E. (1959). *Measurement and evaluation in physical education.* Dubuque: Wm. C. Brown

46. United States Volleyball Association (1967). *Annual Official Volleyball Rules and Reference Guide of the U.S. Volleyball Association.* Berne, IN: USVBA Printer

Index

LaVergne, TN USA
29 November 2009

165467LV00013B/38/A